Managing
Mavericks

Managing Mavericks

The Art of Sales Management

Leslie J. Ades

McGraw-Hill, Inc.

New York   St. Louis   San Francisco   Auckland   Bogotá
Caracas   Lisbon   London   Madrid   Mexico   Milan
Montreal   New Delhi   Paris   San Juan   São Paulo
Singapore   Sydney   Tokyo   Toronto

Library of Congress Cataloging-in-Publication Data

Ades, Leslie J.
    Managing mavericks : the art of sales management / Leslie J. Ades.
        p.   cm.
    Includes index.
    ISBN 0-07-000360-2
    1. Sales management.   I. Title.
    HF5438.4.A33   1992
    658.8′1—dc20   92-7093
                                                          CIP

1 2 3 4 5 6 7 8 9 0   DOC/DOC   9 8 7 6 5 4 3 2

ISBN 0-07-000360-2

The sponsoring editor for this book was James H. Bessent, Jr., the editing supervisor was Jane Palmieri, and the production supervisor was Pamela Pelton. It was set in Baskerville by McGraw-Hill's Professional Book Group composition unit.

Printed and bound by R. R. Donnelley & Sons Company.

*To my darling wife Dorothy,
my guardian angel*

About the Author

Leslie J. Ades is a well-known author, educator, and business consultant. Mr. Ades was formerly vice president of marketing for a Whittaker Corporation subsidiary, national marketing manager for Encyclopaedia Britannica, and district sales manager for Bell & Howell Company, before founding his own marketing consulting and sales training firm in Los Angeles. He brings more than a quarter century of frontline selling and sales management experience to *Managing Mavericks*. His clientele includes: Ace Medical Company, AICPA, the American Management Association, Ampex, California CPA Society, State of California— Department of Conservation, Greyhound Financial Corporation, Honeywell, Kennedy-Wilson, Kevex Corp., Mayo Labs, PIA, Proprietary Computer Systems, Re/Max of California, United Insurance Co., Weiser/Falcon Locks, and Wiltron Corp.

In addition to conducting sales training programs for private industry and numerous state CPA societies, Mr. Ades was formerly a faculty member of the UCLA Graduate School of Management, Pepperdine University Graduate School of Business, and California State University. In 1981 Harper & Row published his first book entitled *Increasing Your Sales Potential*, and he has been a prolific author of articles for *The CPA Journal* and other professional publications.

Contents

2. Psychological Profiling of Mavericks   18

3. From Maverick to President: A Profiling Exercise   35

Preface

For most of my life I have been fascinated by the leadership phenomenon—or lack of it—in business management. In looking over most modern-day companies, we can honestly say that we've had more than our fair share of leaders, both bad ones and good ones. As a perpetual student of sales management, I have noted the dramatic impact of leadership upon the success of a business enterprise.

With the recent resurgence of interest in western themes, the maverick salesperson comes to mind. Most sales executives view these quick-draw artists as independent loners who can make or break their organization. These hotshots can strike it rich with one big bonanza order, but their mercurial behavior can cause stress, divorce, and short circuiting of management careers.

Managing Mavericks is the ultimate challenge for the new and aspiring sales manager. Firm leadership and creative imagination are required to transform these high-plains drifters into a winning sales team. In this book, I shall be discussing sales management from a leadership perspective with particular emphasis on attracting, supervising, and retaining that elusive will-of-the-wisp called maverick.

Up to this point in business history, there's very little material, published or unpublished, on sales management leadership or on managing the maverick salesperson. This book will fill that void. Along this treacherous trail, I'll be sharing a quarter century of frontline sales management experience. Time-proven suggestions will be made on how to meet this supreme leadership challenge and improve your prospects for career growth and development. Humorous anecdotes, salty western lingo, and verbal-proof stories are mixed into a potent success brew, along with ivory tower theory and generous doses of horse sense. If you can apply the down-home precepts of *Managing Mavericks* to your own career situation, you'll be able to ride tall in the saddle and find your own home on the range.

Acknowledgments

This book is the summation of nearly three decades of frontline selling, sales training, and sales management experience. As a business consultant, teacher, and seminar leader, I have been most fortunate to have interfaced with a wide variety of people in leadership positions and been exposed to their goals and challenges. In writing this volume, I have used many of these situations to illustrate key concepts through verbal-proof stories and anecdotes.

In addition to these real-world sales management dilemmas, a number of very fine people helped to shape the final end-product. Special thanks are due to Mary Beth Maher for introducing my manuscript to McGraw-Hill. Without her persistent promotional efforts, this book would never have seen the literary light of day.

Credit for my successful use of western lingo is due entirely to N. R. Shelley who coached and guided me. The old cowpoke certainly knew his stuff.

I am particularly indebted to James H. Bessent, Jr., my sponsoring editor at McGraw-Hill, for his confidence in this project, his professional guidance, and his incisive comments. This was the finest symbiotic relationship of my writing career.

Finally, I want to thank my wonderful wife Dorothy for her acute judgment, loving patience, critical insight, and unflagging emotional support throughout all of my writing endeavors. She not only provided the positive climate necessary for working on this book but also gave me most valuable editorial assistance.

Leslie J. Ades
Los Angeles, California

Introduction

Managing salespeople who are geographically dispersed is a tough enough task, but managing maverick salespeople is the ultimate challenge. According to a well-known dictionary, a *maverick* is "an unbranded range animal, an independent individual who refuses to conform with the group, an independent-minded person who refuses to abide by the dictates of, or resists adherence to, the group; a dissenter." Can you think of a better description of a veteran supersalesperson who is also an organizational misfit? They are a rare breed of talented "loners" who ride their sales territories solo, without needing to be "branded" by their sales managers as part of *any* sales team. But neither are they macho gunslingers who shoot from the hip without aiming. No, this book deals with how to realistically approach managing the activities of these free spirits—these renegades—and their elusive selling behavior. Nobody—but *nobody*—controls them. They can make or break your sales force, as well as your own management career.

Your job is to mold this motley bunch of mavericks into a cohesive selling unit. You were probably a little mavericky yourself or you would not have qualified to be their boss. Now you've got to leave those outlaw ways behind and start thinking and acting like a leader. Your range-riding days are over. *Whatever got you into sales management is no longer good enough to keep you there.* The times are a-changing. Most new sales managers don't last more than four years on the ranch before they are put out to pasture. Some are fired for incompetency; others become stressed out or choose to go back into the field as salespeople— usually for another company. It's "up and out" for them, and a tragic loss of human resources for the firm that promoted them to this slippery position in the first place.

1

Will you be one of those four-year management casualties? Will you get bushwhacked by your competition, or "done in" by your own mavericks? How badly do you really want this position? Are you willing to put all your cards on the table and make a full career commitment? Sales management is not for everyone, certainly not for the faint-hearted. Sales managers ride alone too. Not all of their decisions are popular, or successful. They typically learn their craft the hard way—through blunder and experience. There are no formal schools for aspiring sales managers, but Boot Hill is filled with expired dropouts.

This chronicle of the Old West penetrates the sales maverick mystique and gives you guidelines for controlling their behavior. It is your survival guide for managing mavericks and not being stampeded by them. It will help you develop the requisite skills and management perspectives which will enable you to become a more effective leader while extending your job longevity and enhancing your peace of mind. In these worthy endeavors, your author would like to wish you every possible success.

PART 1

The Leadership Dimensions of Sales Management

To do our fellow men the most good in our power, we must lead where we can, follow where we cannot, and still go with them watching always the favorable moment for helping them to another step.

THOMAS JEFFERSON

1

Sales Managers with the Right Stuff

Every French soldier carries a marshal's baton in his knapsack.
NAPOLEON BONAPARTE

Introduction to Leadership

Why were you selected for the position of sales manager from among your peers? Simply because you demonstrated leadership qualities that other mavericks in your company lacked. I would like to think that every salesperson, if given a chance and guidance, has the potential for taking up the baton of leadership, but you were the chosen one. You had the humility to prepare yourself for this heroic role and must now have the courage to bring it off. Since most sales managers don't last more than four years on the job, you are going to need all the help you can get.

Sales Management Leadership

Leadership is the essence of modern sales management. It reconciles and utilizes different abilities, viewpoints, attitudes, and ideas in the

5

performance of group tasks and organizational missions. It is the ability to inspire other salespeople to work together as a team, following your lead, to attain a common objective whether it is introducing a new product line or service package, increasing sales in a targeted market, or opening up new channels of distribution. When managing mavericks, this is easier said than done.

The Difference between Doing and Managing

No one person can do it all alone, others must want to follow you. How do you get results through other people, when you are used to getting the job done yourself? You were good at it too. That's part of the reason why you're here. But now you've got to step back and let others do the selling job for you, under your patient supervision. This is called *delegation*, the crucial difference between doing and managing.

Moses as Maverick

The first mention of the delegation principle occurs in the Bible. In Exodus, Moses succeeded in liberating the Hebrew slaves from Egyptian bondage, but Pharaoh changed his mind. The Egyptian army pursued the Hebrews to the very edge of the Red Sea, and all seemed lost as Moses hesitated. Finally, his PR agent suggested that if Moses could get God to part the Red Sea for their escape, it would be worth several paragraphs in the Bible.

Once on the other side, Moses took things into his own hands and made all the decisions, both large and small, domestic and international. As he grew weary, his father-in-law Jethro suggested that the people be divided into groups of thousands, hundreds, fifties, and tens and then Moses could select a judge to preside over each group and make the appropriate judgments. When a difficult decision was to be made, it could be referred upward to the next highest level of judge. This would lighten the leadership burden, reduce stress, and free more time for advanced planning and strategy. (Exodus 18:17–23)

In modern management terminology this dilemma is called *executive capacity* and deals with a manager's span of attention and span of effective control. For example, how many mavericks can you physically supervise in the field while you are actively engaged in long-range planning and decision making? This encompasses goal setting, establishing priorities, and the skillful delegation of responsibilities. You must now develop an organization rather than accounts, salespeople rather than, sales, and profits rather than sales volume. Although you are ultimately accountable for overall results, you must delegate responsibility and commensurate authority to your individual sales team members. Even Moses couldn't do his job alone. He needed help. Sorry chums, divine help does not come with your new territory.

Administrative Skills Are Required

Because there is a direct relationship between company profits and effective sales management, the cost of operating a sales force is usually the single largest marketing expense of an industrial company. One of the criteria upon which your job performance will be evaluated is your administrative ability. Successful administration rests upon three essential skills: technical, human, and conceptual.

Technical Skills

Technical skills are an understanding of, and proficiency in, a specific kind of activity; particularly one involving methods, processes, procedures, or techniques.

Selling skills are your technical skills. You have mastered the art of selling, developed accounts, and managed a territory. You know how to create and maintain a customer base. You are technically qualified for the position of sales manager.

However, if you have never sold anything to anybody, how can you expect to be any good at leading other salespeople? You can fool the people above you in an organization, but you can never fool the people below you. The mavericks will eat you alive! They know what you're supposed to do, even if you don't.

A perfect example of this situation is illustrated by a salesperson who submitted her expense account to her inexperienced sales manager with a $500 hat on it. Since she called on "high-fashion" accounts in the Manhattan garment district, she felt justified in charging the hat to the company. Her sales manager objected, stating that personal expenses were not "allowable" and that she should delete it from her expense account. The savvy salesperson did not object and duly submitted her next month's expense account on time and perfectly in order. There was a footnote at the bottom which stated: "The hat's in there. See if you can find it!"

Another important part of sales management leadership is coaching and training. You can no more teach a subject that you don't know than you can lead a person to a place that you've never been. It simply cannot be done. As an experienced salesperson, you have pounded the pavement and paid your dues. You've already been there and have acquired the technical selling skills to prove it.

Technical Skills Give You Source Credibility

Without actual front-line selling experience you cannot command respect or have any kind of source credibility among subordinates. On the other hand, if you have selling experience but were indifferent to time and territory management and the administrative aspects of your job, how can you ever aspire to manage other salespeople? You must learn how to manage yourself first, before you are qualified to manage others.

Sometimes Our Technical Skills Get in the Way

Some would-be sales managers are so good at selling—so used to *doing*—that they are either irreplaceable in the field or cannot make the transition from selling to managing. A prime illustration of this leadership failure is the story of Richard the Lion-Hearted, the original "Poor Richard" of English history.

Coeur de Lion as Maverick

Richard was a great warrior but a disastrous king—a muddling medieval maverick. Of course he could chop and slice with the best of them and was very popular with the troops. But, as the newly appointed leader of the kingdom, he couldn't give up being a soldier. So off he went to fight in the Crusades—which at that time had a fairly low priority in his realm—and left England to get into deeper and deeper trouble. The capital appropriations he made to the Crusades were ridiculously high and were desperately needed for other parts of the economy. The end result of his superb technical skill was disaster—imprisonment for himself in Austria and brother John's usurpation of his throne in England.

There are many Coeur de Lions in sales management today. They are the unfortunate mavericks who cannot let go of selling because that is their main comfort zone. Paperwork and the administrative side of management is definitely not for them. They always want to go back out into the field, where the real action is. As a result, these doers are either fired for incompetence, burn out within four years, or choose to return to the field as a regular salesperson.

Conceptual Skills

Conceptual skills involve your ability to view your company as a whole which is much greater than the sum of its parts. They include recognizing how the various functions of the organization depend upon each other and how changes in one part affect all the others.

As a member of your firm's middle management team you must broaden your departmental perspective to include the bigger corporate picture. Although your job performance will be appraised by the successful attainment of sales volume goals, they are clearly subordinate to, and supportive of, overall corporate goals. The sales realization plan is only one of several concurrent marketing strategies which enable a firm to achieve the long-range objectives of its business plan. Figure 1-1 gives you a conceptual view of a business enterprise.

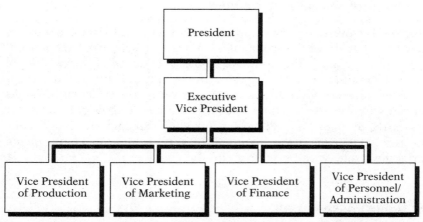

Figure 1-1. Conceptual view of a typical company. The conceptual view advocates the division of a company into four separate but equal functions which are integrated and coordinated by the executive vice president to achieve the long-range objectives of the firm's business plan. The business plan flows from the mission statement and top-echelon philosophy and intent of the business enterprise.

Forget your former free-wheeling ways as a sales rep. If you are ever going to succeed as a sales manager, your perspective must be reoriented as follows:

1. *Profitable sales rather than just sales volume per se.* Try to be more attentive to profitable differences among different product and/or service lines and customer classes. Sales volume increases and inventory turnover will not always make up for losses in profitability. Ignore the optimistic maverick who asserts: "We're losing a buck on each unit, but don't worry, Boss. We'll make it up on the volume!"

2. *Long-term market planning instead of short-term tactics.* Think about product and/or service and market-segment strategies over the next three to five years. Where do you, as a company, want to be at that time? What position do you want to have in the marketplace? How does that compare with the place which you presently occupy?

3. *Market segments viewed as a whole entity rather than limited to individual customers or key accounts.* Use your intimate knowledge about these accounts and the reasons why they buy from your firm to identify market factors that can be used to replicate that success in other segments.

4. *Emphasis on desk work — administration — as opposed to field work.* Develop plans and strategies which can be implemented by others, instead of becoming involved personally. Progress from a doer to a manager and a leader. Become a dexterous desk jockey rather than an aimless range rider.

Figure 1-2 presents a conceptual view of a typical firm's marketing department. It shows that your sales team is a subset, or the action unit, of the strategic marketing unit. All of the activities of each operational unit, or subset in the marketing department, must be integrated and coordinated to serve your firm's customers on a cost-effective basis. As you can see, the sales tail does not wag the marketing dog. Don't get it backwards, or Boot Hill will beckon for your managerial carcass. Your maverick sales team is the hit squad of your company. They execute marketing strategy under your artful direction.

The Hidden-Agenda Trap

A lack of conceptual skills causes some sales managers and other executives to fall into the hidden-agenda trap, or the harboring of ulterior motives. Consider this scenario: The CEO sends down from the corporate mountaintop a new policy or plan. Immediately every department

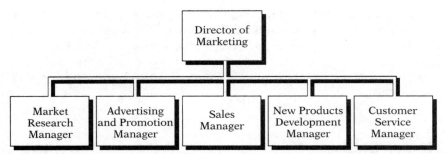

Figure 1-2. Conceptual view of a typical marketing department. The marketing concept strives to achieve overall company goals by determining the needs and wants of target markets and delivering customer satisfaction more effectively than competitors. It is an overall strategy which is designed to plan, price, promote, and distribute want-satisfying goods and services to present and potential customers. All subsets, or tactical units, of the marketing department must be coordinated with and integrated into this overall strategy of profitably creating and maintaining satisfied customers. The sales realization plan is part of the overall marketing plan and subject to its direction.

head in the conference room turns around and has a meeting with their "invisible committee," which usually stands behind them at these important meetings. This furtive dialogue is short and sweet and directly to the point: "How does this new policy affect my bonus?" That's it, nothing more. What else matters? The dialogue ends, and unshakable positions are now taken by all parties. If this new policy affects your bonus or position in the firm in a positive manner — such as, you're going to have more salespeople, a bigger incentive plan, etc. — you are going to support it with all your heart. You're going to go on public record stating what a brilliant idea it is and how you will give this new plan your undying support.

But what if this new corporate policy will affect your bonus in a negative way? Or reduce your stature in the organization? For instance, you need to make quota this quarter, but quality-control problems have put a "hold" on all shipments until these problems are corrected. Your bonus is tied to orders *shipped,* not booked. What are you going to say to your CEO now? You *know* that you are going to be flat out against this new policy and fight it until your last breath.

A third possibility is that this new policy has no effect on your precious bonus one way or the other. What do you do now? Why of course you become political and drift any old way that the corporate winds of fortune are blowing. The lack of conceptual skills exacerbates your lack of direction.

Thus hidden agendas are the underlying currents of passive resistance to long-term change when short-term self-interests are at stake. Executives with a conceptual view of their total business and their careers know that they don't have to win every battle in order to win the war and that the contributions of all company departments are necessary in winning and keeping clients. These executives know that job satisfaction is helping their customers get what they want and that their own job security lies in seeing that they do. Even a prairie dog knows that.

Human Skills

Human skills are your ability to work effectively as a group member and build cooperative effort within your sales team.

Most successful salespeople excel in this crucial area, having established good interpersonal relationships with a variety of diverse customer personalities, distributors, home office personnel, and so on, during the course of their selling careers. You probably belonged to a few professional associations, yourself, and perhaps held elected offices. Most mavericks know how to bring home the bacon and be popular with the ranch hands who can expedite their payroll checks or expedite deliveries to their most important clients. (Some folks think that these mavericks are a little bit too expert at cultivating these internal relationships.)

Now that you are at the sales management level, however, these human skills must be broadened to encompass working relationships with other middle-management executives as well as your superiors. You are now a member of your firm's executive team and must represent their interests *downward* to your subordinates. At the same time, as leader of your sales team, you must also advocate their interests *upward* to your fellow management-echelon peers. No easy job. You are the man or woman in the middle, and your human skills will be tested as they were never tested before.

For example, you will be obliged to interface, on an almost daily basis, with executives who have direct or indirect power over you and whose personalities turn you off. Your corporate economist probably doesn't have enough personality to be an accountant, but his or her forecasts affect the size of your budget. If you want more funds to hire additional salespeople or contest money, do not tell your chief financial officer (who is most likely a CPA) the story, which is currently circulating the Pentagon Building in Washington, D.C., alleging that a CPA invented the neutron bomb—it kills all the people but leaves the assets intact! Don't expect everybody to appreciate that kind of maverick humor, because they just might not. Pity.

A Change of Focus Is Needed

The focus of your human skills expertise must also *change from developing accounts to developing your salespeople.* Your Lone Ranger days are over. Your task is to develop team action, not individual action. You must create a working environment where each individual maverick will feel that he or she is an important member of a winning team and will be spurred on by personal pride and peer pressure to maximum achievement. You can facilitate this developmental process by doing the following:

1. *Help your subordinates plan.* Everything begins with planning, but most mavericks rely on intuition and "gut feel." Their success is usually based on an uncanny feeling for situations and personalities, a willingness to explore the unknown and to sense selling possibilities and implications that are not readily apparent, and a reliance on an instinctive kind of logical process whose steps are often hidden in their unconscious mind. As you can see, getting these proud individuals to sit down and plan their work is a formidable challenge indeed.

2. *Work with your mavericks in setting goals for which* they *will be held responsible.* This requires the establishment of achievement targets within specific time frames. If you can't get these independent-minded souls to plan, how are you ever going to get them focused on the right targets? Again, shaping them up is one of your most important chores.

3. *Give them assistance in attaining these goals through training, coaching, and counseling.* Effective sales managers are teachers, advisers, and consultants to their mavericks. Teach them everything you know so that you can narrow the odds of success in their favor. This is one of the soundest ways of winning their confidence and respect.

4. *Give them enough freedom of action to achieve, which involves delegation.* Give these thoroughbreds their heads along with enough authority to get the job done and make the inevitable blunders. Create the kind of open organizational environment where everyone feels free to admit to an honest mistake without fear of unfair reprisal. As long as your mavericks come to you with a plan to remedy the damage, they should have your full and unwavering support.

5. *Hold them accountable for the results of their actions.* This is a function of performance appraisals. How can you evaluate performance if you have not established previously agreed-upon objectives and appraisal criteria?

You must develop your motley assortment of mavericks into a cohesive team of sales professionals who share common goals while working independently on different tasks under your overall direction. Let's face it, mavericks are very talented individuals with specific jobs to do, and they could perform those jobs without having to be part of *any* sales team. Getting them to work together and also achieve organizational goals is your supreme human-skills challenge as a sales manager.

Administrative Skills Summary

The clock is ticking. If you want to survive on the job for more than the four-year norm, you must learn how to delegate and develop the three essential administrative skills as outlined in this chapter. You need:

1. Sufficient *technical skills* to accomplish the planning and implementation of your duties and responsibilities in a timely fashion. This is the paperwork side of sales management.

2. Keen *conceptual skills* to recognize and integrate the key company departmental interrelationships and the various organizational factors which affect your leadership situation. This will expand your executive capacity and improve your decision-making ability to the maximum benefit to you and the entire company. It will also open up other vistas for your career growth and progress.

3. Adroit *human skills* to build a successful sales team while working effectively with your fellow middle-management peers and top-echelon bosses. These are the human relations and political aspects of your job position.

The relative importance of these three skills will vary with the level of administrative responsibility and the culture of your company. Our focus in this book will be primarily on *human skills* because your ultimate success or failure as a sales manager rests on your ability to manage mavericks. You must put the right people into the right places so that your organizational objectives can be reached on a consistent basis. This does not mean that the other important aspects of the job will be completely ignored. To the contrary, some will be treated in considerable depth.

The Administrative Trap

Although we have discussed the importance of administrative skills in effective sales-force management, it can be carried to excess. Some misguided sales managers view their jobs in purely administrative terms. Once promoted to this lofty position, some feel that they've got it made in the shade and that all they have to do now is to ensconce themselves by the fireside in their comfortable offices, dole out the leads and grow rich on their override commissions. If this description fits you and your fantasies about your leadership role, then you're going to be in for a rude awakening. Your mavericks will see to that! You've got to earn their respect and set an honest example for your staff to follow.

Set an Honest Example

No salesperson worth his or her drawing account wants an "inside" administrator for a boss. Set an example, an honest example for your mavericks to emulate. If you spend a lot of time hanging around the office drinking coffee, so will they. If you spend too much time on the telephone, so will they. Don't ask your mavericks to do anything that you cannot do or have never done. They will never respect you. At appropriate times you must go back out into the field — where the action is — and lead the cattle drive.

If your leadership is successful, it will create a momentum in your organization which will empower your mavericks with such a feeling of pride and energy that they will produce results which you and they would never have thought possible. Your decisiveness and active involvement in their professional welfare will instill confidence in your leadership and set a positive example for all of your subordinates to imitate.

Champion of Champions

As previously stated, a sales manager is a top executive in a firm's marketing department. He or she is in charge of the company's personal selling function. A sales manager's main responsibility is to increase profitable sales volume on an annualized basis. The Official Maverick Definition of a Sales Manager, however, differs considerably. You can find it scrawled on every fence post from the hills of Montana to the gorges of the Texas Panhandle. It reads as follows:

A sales manager is the s.o.b. from the home office with the extra 5%.

This is the bigshot with the checkbook who arrives at the eleventh hour of a deadlocked client-vendor negotiation and closes the deal by offering the buyer an extra 5 percent price concession. Now, any old polecat could do that! If mavericks had that kind of latitude in pricing, they could have corralled those orders all by themselves, without any "divine" intervention from the home office.

Most mavericks think that a sales manager is about as useless as a water moccasin on a buffalo hunt, and about as dangerous. Although proud, creative, and independent, mavericks can be as stubborn as mules. These ornery critters are so cocky and rebellious that they love to relate this story about their bothersome bosses:

> A hungry dude strode through the swinging doors of a local meat market and inquired about the price of brains for his forthcoming fancy chuck wagon–cookout party.
>
> The proprietor quickly responded, "Calves' brains are ten dollars a pound, mavericks' brains are one hundred dollars a pound, but sales managers' brains are one thousand dollars a pound."
>
> The astonished customer asked, "Why so much money for sales managers' brains?"
>
> The nonchalant butcher replied, "You've got to kill a lot of sales managers to get enough brains!"

That's how mavericks view authority figures. These rambunctious reps are usually sales superstars but organizational misfits. They prefer the wide-open spaces and would rather ramble aimlessly around the range than be hog-tied and branded as a conforming member of any sales team. Managing ordinary salespeople is a tough enough assignment, but managing mavericks can be the pits.

Remember, sales managers don't capture market share all by themselves, their sales force does. Your success and job security depends upon the continuous productivity and cooperation of all members of your sales team. Without it, you won't have a snowball's chance in hell of surviving on the job. You see, sales management is like a huge human rodeo where a variety of bucking broncos must be ridden until they're broken in and domesticated. You sit on the slipperiest seat in the company, but if you can hang in there and not get thrown for a loop, you deserve all the glory and the accolades. Sales management is not for the thin-skinned, saddle sore, or faint-hearted. It's for the champion of champions! Whether you're a dude or a dudette, your work is certainly cut out for you.

Chapter 1 Roundup

No sales manual, videocassette training film, computer game, or textbook could ever take the place of good proactive sales management leadership. So I urge you to reach into your knapsack, take out your marshal's baton, and start using it today. It was no accident that you were chosen for the job—you've got the right stuff, and now is your chance to prove it. The stirring words of Sir Winston Churchill will inspire you in this new leadership challenge: "I felt as if I were walking with Destiny, and that all my past life had been but a preparation for this hour and for this trial."

2
Psychological Profiling of Mavericks

Nothing great will ever be achieved without great men, and men are great only if they are determined to be so. CHARLES DE GAULLE

Introduction to Psychological Profiling

As the great French leader implied, *leadership is an attitude,* a state of mind with vision that is capable of foreseeing and acting upon potential problems which are germane to the enterprise.

Sales management leadership is 90 percent attitude and 10 percent aptitude. Anyone who wants to be a leader can become one, given the requisite technical skills and the willingness to make a full commitment.

The Sales Management Grid

The sales management grid is a graphic illustration of a sales manager's attitude toward managing mavericks. Most newly appointed sales managers want to be popular with their salespeople and bosses but know that their job performance will be judged by order production. They don't

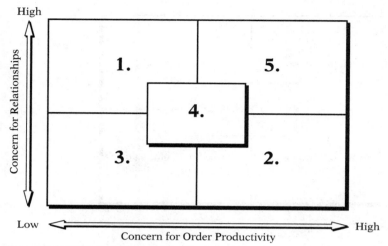

Figure 2-1. The sales management grid.

want to be too hard on their mavericks, but they must get results or they will be history. This is their dilemma. The sales management grid as shown in Fig. 2-1 illustrates these two concerns and a range of possible interactions. How sales managers reconcile these conflicting concerns is determined by their attitudes and reflected in their leadership styles.

The positions above the midpoint on the horizontal axis indicate a high concern for relationships, while those below indicate low concern. The positions to the right of the midpoint of the vertical axis indicate concern for order production, while those to the left indicate relative low concern, or relative indifference. Where the two axes meet is the center of the grid, the middle ground or compromise position.

Psychological Profiling of Mavericks

Each of the five basic positions on the grid represents a personality type. Mavericks and sales managers alike fall into one of these types. As such, they act out their roles in a unique and consistent manner according to their personality characteristics and psychological needs. However, most sales personnel do not fit neatly into any one style but are a mixture of more than one behavioral model. You may see something of each style in your own role behavior at different times and under different circumstances. To complicate matters further, most mavericks have a "backup" style (which they use when under pressure or during a crisis) that might be completely different when their dominant power style fails.

Psychological profiling through the use of trait casting can order the

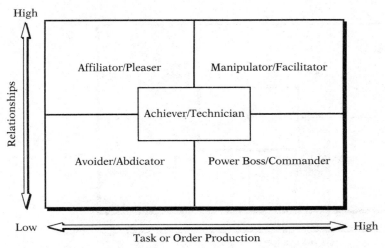

Figure 2-2. Psychological profiling of mavericks on the sales management grid.

social field for you and thereby give you valuable insights into the diverse personalities of your mavericks, customers, fellow managers, and even superiors.

Most sales managers, as well as mavericks, have a dominant style of role behavior. Figure 2-2 illustrates that role behavior by positioning each personality type on the sales management grid.

How to Use This Typology of Personality Types

Many psychologists strongly reject the use of typologies—classifications of people based upon personality types—such as the models presented in this chapter. They argue that typologies encourage the view of people as stereotypes rather than as individuals. This may be true to a certain extent, but typologies are extremely important in communicating with and analyzing individuals and should be used as flexible, open tools. They will help you develop a sensitivity toward people which will serve you well in your business career. These typology types apply not only to you but to the mavericks whom you will be managing. In other words, this material pertains to the *managed,* as well as the *manager.* You will never look at people the same way after reading this chapter as you did beforehand.

For each type, I will start with a general description. Then, for purposes of illustration, I will compare the various types with regard to two of the most visible manifestations of personality—one's office and one's car. Admittedly, this is only half serious, so have some fun categorizing some of your colleagues and acquaintances. On the serious side, however, keep in mind that this exercise will help you understand and deal more effectively with a broad spectrum of people. Let's begin with the erstwhile stereotype of a typical salesperson, the affiliator/pleaser.

1. Affiliator/Pleaser

In the upper left-hand quadrant of the sales management grid is the affiliator/pleaser, who has an inordinately high concern for relationships but a very low concern for order production. This cheerful, laissez-faire personality type emphasizes sociability, harmony, and togetherness. Their underlying assumption is that people will perform miracles for someone they like. As sales managers, affiliators believe, for example, that by being pleasant and not demanding of their salespeople they can stimulate them to work effectively. Their philosophy of managing people is "Whatever the gang wants, let 'em have it! They're good people, they know what they are doing. Why bug 'em?"

Behavioral Characteristics

Eager to be liked and accepted as one of the gang, this amiable personality type plays down all differences in rank and is readily accessible and very sensitive to the feelings of others. Because of his or her great affiliation need, the affiliator relates well to others and is a joiner, team player, follower, and compromiser. These fun people are the cheerleaders of your organization. They're the ones most likely to bring cookies to the office. They belong to every popular association in town, but usually in a number-two position. Leadership roles are definitely not their forte because leaders must make decisions and not all decisions are popular. Since they feel that it is very important to be liked and popular, affiliators will usually avoid making unpopular decisions of any kind.

These enthusiastic executives are the number-one office gossips, knowing all the "juicy stuff," such as who's sleeping with whom and who's working on what job assignments. They pride themselves on being the best source of "insider" information and on being known by all of the maître d's in Beverly Hills. Their favorite topics of conversation also include team spectator sports and the latest fashions but certainly *not* business as they don't like facts or figures—too boring!

The Affiliator's Office Is Friendly

The affiliator's office is cheerful and comfortable, with all kinds of toys—to please everyone—on the desk. Even if the affiliator is a nonsmoker, an ashtray is available for guests. The surrounding walls are laden with trophies, awards, and autographed photos of famous sports figures and celebrities—usually shaking hands with them. It is not *what* they know that counts, but *who* knows them that is really important. They are fond of cute sayings, cartoons, and bumper stickers. Data are conspicuous by their absence, and the furniture is so comfortable that you feel like staying there all day.

The Affiliator's Car Is Popular

Naturally it would be the most popular model with the affiliator's peer group or the group with whom she or he would like to be affiliated. If it isn't a "Beamer" (BMW) or a van, it would probably be a flashy red sports car—that is, if it wouldn't offend anybody at the office. (As you can see, there is a little bit of avoidance behind that friendly facade.) Nevertheless, customized license plates are a must.

Male Affiliator   Female Affiliator

Affiliator/Pleaser Analysis

In moderate situational control situations, affiliator/pleaser sales managers tend to be at their best and can achieve better than average results. Although they do not relate well to facts and figures (they are terrible at paperwork) these jovial folks seek to alleviate anxiety and tension in their group, mediate conflict well, and are patient and able to handle creative decision-making groups. They are considerate and very much concerned with the feelings and opinions of their sales team members. They are more cheerleaders than business leaders, and are sometimes perceived as congenial pushovers by their mavericks.

2. Power Boss/Commander

In the lower right-hand corner of the grid is the power boss/commander, who believes that nothing matters as much as getting the job done. Unlike the affiliator/pleaser, the feelings of people don't count, only results, and the job better be done right. Their outspoken philosophy is "It's *my way*, or the highway! We'll make quota, even if it kills you!" They believe in the Golden Rule: He or she who has the gold, makes the rules.

Known for their aggressive and domineering behavior, these autocrats are brash, intolerant, sexist, and rigid but are intuitive leaders. The power boss sales manager tends to believe that all salespeople are born lazy and are naturally apathetic and uncooperative. Therefore they believe that their mavericks must be constantly whipped into shape, driven, and tightly controlled. They are firmly convinced that only hard-nosed managers get results and to delegate is a sign of weakness.

Behavioral Characteristics

Power bosses don't lead, they command. They have all the sensitivity of a bull moose in heat, and kicking butt is their favorite means of communication. "The firings will continue until morale improves!" is a favorite saying. They are *always* right, must win in every negotiation, and have a huge ego but a strong aversion to facts and figures. "Don't confuse me with facts and figures, my mind's made up. Now do it!" is a typical power boss response to a logical presentation. Because they are technically insecure, their emotions lead them to make snap judgments based on gut feelings; they will not share credit, even if it is someone else's idea. Guess who gets the blame, though, if the idea fails?

When enraged, they've been known to throw things around the office. Power bosses are legends in their own minds and feel that the whole world is entitled to their opinions, which they do not hesitate to give at the drop of a hat. Their idea of a motivational appeal comes in two forms, one positive and the other negative.

A positive power boss appeal: "If you do a good job this week, you get to keep it."

A negative power boss appeal: "If you screw up this assignment, you've got two weeks and jolly good luck!"

The Power Boss's Office Is Awesome

If the office of the typical power boss were designed to be large enough to contain his or her huge ego, it would have to be a miniature replica of New York's Grand Central Station perched atop the executive suite with a corner window view of the city skyline. Nothing else would be remotely acceptable. The interior is dark and forbidding. There is absolutely nothing on the walls or on the massive wooden desk except a squawk box and a gold-plated, matching, executive pen-and-pencil set. Oh yes, there might be a gun collection or pictures of the Persian Gulf War bombing scenes around. Sometimes there is a large picture of the power boss or of his or her idol — someone like General George S. Patton or Margaret Thatcher — hanging from a prominent wall at eye level.

Power bosses sit on a thronelike chair which is directly in front of a large window with venetian blinds which are slanted so that the sun's rays blind all visitors. While silhouetted in this regal posture, there are four possible seating arrangements for their unfortunate visitors:

1. All of the other chairs in the room have an inch sawed off the bottom of their legs so that the power boss can tower over you in an ominous manner.

2. All of the other chairs are placed at the rear of the room and are nailed to the floor. A space vacuum is thus created which causes the power boss to complain loudly, "Speak up! I can't hear you. What's a matter, are you a wimp, or something?"

3. There might be a rickety, three-legged stool that seems to be on the verge of collapsing under your weight. Since you don't know when you're going to wind up on the floor, you're always nervous and apprehensive in a power boss's presence.

4. My favorite power boss guest chair is the plush, upholstered love seat with a leather cover. It comes in two varieties. The first one is so firm that it is rather uncomfortable. Everything seems fine until you settle in, and then shift position. Then the chair makes a noise like you are passing wind! The other variety of this chair comes with such a soft support that you sink so deeply into the seat that your knees are higher than your eyeballs. This is the supplicant's posture, and you appear to be begging for favors.

If you smoke, a power boss will offer you a cigarette and then watch you squirm when you realize that there aren't any ashtrays in the room. This volatile managerial type is a master of the stress interview and believes that it is better to give (ulcers) than to receive. Winning through intimidation is the name of the game, and it even extends to their personal automobile.

The Power Boss's Car Is Impressive

Since he or she always "buys American," flies the flag, and believes in apple pie and motherhood, you know that this chauvinist would only drive an American car. What is the biggest and most powerful

American-made car? One that is so big that it needs hinges so that it can negotiate corners? Naturally it would be a black, stretch Lincoln Continental which is fully loaded. Besides the dark-tinted windows, wet bar, TV, and speed radar set, there are *two* telephones. Why two? Simply because the power boss wants you to know that the other is ringing so that your conversation can be abruptly terminated. One line must be kept open in case the President or a member of Congress wants to talk to him or her on some urgent matter.

These pompous people love to park in handicapped parking spaces or loading zones and are fond of personalized license plates. Since they are very direct people, these plates are easy to spot.

Power Boss/Commander Analysis

Despite these lovable shortcomings, power bosses do perform best in crisis situations and low-control situations because of their decisiveness and strong task orientation. In troubleshooting situations where a firm hand and a no-nonsense attitude are required to get the operation moving, they excel. Power bosses can be very loyal, produce superb results over the short term, and are probably natural-born leaders. They are also the easiest people to handle, once you get over your fear of them.

3. Avoider/Abdicator

Here, in the lower-left quadrant, low concern for order production is coupled with low concern for people. There is no leadership dilemma here because this manager or rep merely opts for survival on the job. Avoider/abdicators have a great need for safety and security in an ever-changing business environment and fear that close involvement might disrupt the status quo, so they keep it to an absolute minimum.

Behavioral Characteristics

Avoider/abdicators do not like conflict or trouble, are indecisive, insecure, and rarely take chances. They are bureaucratic administrators who provide scant leadership, serving primarily as conduits for orders from higher in the chain of command. They are introverted, have low self-esteem, take few risks, and tend to procrastinate and then rely on corporate policies and procedures to justify their inaction.

When in charge, avoiders ponder, when in doubt they mumble, and when in trouble they delegate—to get rid of the problem. If that doesn't work, they turn the whole matter over to a committee for an annual review. Avoiders are members of every committee imaginable and usually delegate by default. Somebody is always taking away part of their job responsibilities because nothing is happening and deadlines are approaching.

As executives, they are shy, require lots of data—which they file rather than use—and take the longest time of the five personality types to make a decision. Even then, they aren't always sure that it was the right decision after all. Their management philosophy is cautious: "It is far better to do nothing now, than to make a decision which you will later regret." They always need more information and are very inaccessible. "The jury's still out," or they don't have enough information to commit. Avoiders never return your telephone calls or answer your letters but will "carbon copy the world" if an interdepartmental "paper war" ever erupts. It's like dealing with a 500-pound marshmallow: You can beat on it and it gives in, but the damned thing never moves! Sometimes it even absorbs you.

The avoider/abdicator usually brings lunch to work in a brown paper bag and arrives at the office with a bulging briefcase exactly one minute after the boss arrives, and departs precisely one minute before the boss goes home each evening. These carefully designed maneuvers are calculated to show the boss how hard he or she works and how loyal he or she is to the company. Loyal this person is, but upon careful inspection of the tattered briefcase you might notice dust on the locks—a sure sign that the briefcase was never opened.

What's inside the brown paper lunch bag? A thermos bottle filled with decaf coffee and a peanut butter and jelly sandwich—creamy, not chunky. That would pose too great a risk to avoider's dental work.

The Avoider's Office Is Hard to Find

Located in the most remote part of the building, an avoider's office looks like the Yuma, Arizona, branch office of the Wells Fargo Express after a violent sandstorm. Papers and files are scattered all over, and her or his "in" basket and desk drawers are jammed with documents and overdue reports. The "out" basket is bone empty, and the only other chair in the room is covered with data and debris because he or she really doesn't want any visitors hanging around.

The classic avoider's dime-store expendable furniture is arranged in a strategic manner so that the rolltop desk faces the wall—opposite the door—where there's a picture of a window. If a visitor peers in from the hallway, all she or he would see is the back of the avoider's head and a plastic plant. No eye contact is ever established and face-to-face meetings are usually cut short by "urgent" meetings. There might be a picture of Mom on the desk or a favorite pet in a cracked frame buried among the papers. This procrastinator had been planning to do something about that frame, but the pet died two years ago.

The corporate lavatory is the avoider's second office, a sort of "home away from home" where she or he can catch up on serious reading. If you ever find a corporate bathroom strewn with an array of impressive business journals and other publications, you know that a classic avoider is lurking nearby. The avoider's most productive hours are spent here, away from the maddening crowd. While all of the internecine political battles are being fought outside those peaceful walls, he or she sits serenely in unruffled solitude. Finally, when the noise subsides and the smoke clears, the avoider surreptitiously emerges from the toilet, steps carefully over the bodies of fallen comrades, and tries to slink away. But too late: a senior executive spots the avoider and shouts, "Hey, there's old George (Georgia), he's (she's) been around here the longest. Let's give the company presidency to him (her)!" And that's how an avoider gets to be the president. You would be surprised at the number of CEOs who've made it to the top because of attrition.

The Avoider's Car Is Nondescript

Since the avoider doesn't want to be noticed and hates high-pressure confrontations with people, particularly used-car salespeople, he or she becomes an automobile owner in one of two ways. Either the avoider buys a car right off the lot, as is, or his or her spouse makes the decision. A typical avoider's car would not offend anybody and, hopefully, would not even be noticed. What kind of car immediately comes to mind? An American-made automobile with substandard equipment, pea-green color, with only one door that opens, and about seven years old. The AM radio doesn't work (the antenna is broken), and there are rust marks on the doors. When the transmission fails, avoiders will first consider reactivating their bus passes. Avoider license plates are difficult to spot.

Avoider/Abdicator Analysis

Although they have blah personalities and lack charisma and staff involvement, avoider/abdicators are efficient administrators who excel in all routinized sales management activities and high-control leadership situations. They follow instructions faithfully, seldom create conflicts or openly criticize their mavericks, and are sensitive to their weaknesses and problems. Avoiders never rock the corporate boat—that is their secret to success.

Despite their low visibility and weak self-image, somehow their departments always seem to take care of themselves. If handled skillfully, avoiders can become loyal employees and the backbone of the staff—they don't like change. They are the *survivors* of the firm and will probably be there long after most others are gone.

4. Achiever/Technician

The middle of the grid is where intermediate concern for task is linked with only moderate concern for people. These "efficient" sales personnel are basically task-oriented technicians who are alternatively competitive with, and conciliatory to, other mavericks. As managers, many times these number-crunchers have their own sales territories to continuously demonstrate their superior selling and time-management skills.

Behavioral Characteristics

These are "bottom liners": confident, analytical, independent, and relatively insensitive to people. When greeting a sales team member, they only have one question: "Where's the orders?" Like the power bosses, they hate excuses and can be equally abrasive, demanding, and impatient with subordinates while imposing their own personality needs for perfection on them. They are hard-working and driven to prove their self-worth through craft excellence. Unlike the power boss and the affiliator, they thrive on data and use logic in their decision making.

Although the quality of their decision making is superb, it is usually short-range oriented, and the process itself can be quite lengthy, as they may require reams of data before finally acting.

Achievers are so fascinated by the intricate bark configurations on the proverbial tree that they cannot even see its branches, let alone the entire forest. They are excellent project people—sometimes handling a half dozen or more at one time—expert craftspeople and technicians but lacking in conceptual skills. They also have difficulty delegating work assignments because they can always do the job much better themselves. Achievers define delegation as "giving the work to someone who is dumber than you."

Despite their narrow focus and poor people skills, these efficient-minded types are fair-minded and will change their minds when confronted with a superior solution which is based·on documented facts. I once knew an achiever/technician sales manager who fired a sales rep for cheating on his expense account. The sales manager thought that he had made a mistake, but later changed his mind!

The Achiever's Office Is Functional

The achiever's office is a model of functionality. It contains a state-of-the-art collection of information sources and leading-edge office technology, including a desktop computer, fax machine, and the latest telephone system (voice mail, etc.). The desk is spartan but serviceable and surrounded by charts and graphs. A live plant (for oxygen) and a calculator lie on the surface along with the ubiquitous pad and pencil.

The achiever's chair has wheels on it so he or she can have instant access to all the data sources located throughout the room. A few technical awards and a family picture—spouse and 2.3 children—can be found hanging from the walls. The two uncomfortable visitors' chairs have timing devices on them, and there are no ashtrays around. Both the lighting and room temperature are electronically controlled for optimum working conditions and maximum efficiency.

The Achiever's Car Is Efficient

After extensive research, which would include *Consumer Reports, Motor Trend,* and *Car and Driver,* achievers would finally purchase the automobile with the best gas mileage, maintenance record, trade-in value, and overall performance characteristics. Most likely it would be a midrange import with a 10-year warranty. Its color would be neutral to light—high-tech gray or silver—because this vehicle is warmer in the winter (absorbs heat), reflects the summer's heat, and doesn't show the dirt as much as darker colors. A cellular phone is a must, but the other accessories will probably be standard. After all, a car is just a means of transportation—it gets you from one geographic point to another. Achievers often prefer a bicycle because of its cardiovascular benefits. Achiever/technician license plates aren't hard to spot.

Achiever/Technician Analysis

Achiever/technician sales managers are very creative, self-reliant, goal-oriented, and *problem-centered* instead of *self-centered* (like the power boss). They have the courage of their convictions and are not afraid—like the affiliators or avoiders—of making unpopular decisions. Facts will always vindicate their controversial decisions. They would rather be right—based on the data—than President and usually meet or exceed departmental goals ahead of schedule. This is accomplished through a democratic style of leadership whereby their subordinates' talents are fully utilized. Most mavericks find them boring and too businesslike, but they can become the "stars" of the show.

5. Manipulator/Facilitator

In the upper right-hand quadrant of the grid, a high concern for results is coupled with genuine concern for relationships. The classic leadership dilemma is resolved through the skillful manipulation of the business environment and the individuals who are an integral part of it. The effective integration of concern for relationships and concern for order production is achieved by involving others and their ideas in determining the strategies as well as the conditions of work. The process *appears* to be "bottom-up" management, but the reality of the phenomenon might be the exact opposite.

Manipulator/facilitators employ team-building tactics and *participative management* which involves each maverick in problem solving, goal setting, and decision making in matters which affect their territories. There is a high concern for the needs of both the individual salesperson and the attainment of organizational objectives. They and their salespeople function as a well-integrated team rather than a bunch of independent mavericks.

A basic aim of manipulator management is to promote conditions that balance individual creativity, accelerating order productivity, and high morale through concerted team action. It is a highly manipulative leadership technique which requires exceptional technical, conceptual, and human skills. Although gamesmanship is utilized to create "win-win" situations, there are considerable risks involved in applying this leadership power style. It can backfire, with severe ramifications for both the organization and the manipulator's own career progress.

Since acting and manipulating have several things in common, the comments of the late Spencer Tracy are apropos: "Acting is a great profession, as long as you don't get caught doing it." Good manipulators never get caught in the act of manipulating.

Behavioral Characteristics

Manipulator/facilitator sales managers use people and things to get the job done. They accomplish this delicate task by establishing links between personal goals and organizational objectives. These persuasive opportunists are long-term strategists who are extremely perceptive and sensitive to the psychological needs of others. They have greater human skills than the affiliator/pleasers, possess technical skills which far surpass those of achiever/technicians, but also have the conceptual skills which all of the other personality types lack. That is why you will usually find them in the top echelons of most organizations.

These shrewd executives are long-range and goal-oriented, see the "big picture" immediately, and are relatively ego-detached. They play down their real power and don't mind losing every corporate battle because they usually win the war. They are such splendid delegators that sometimes they are mistaken for avoider/abdicators who are out of the action arena. Their outstanding personal attributes are flexibility and resourcefulness. Manipulators have that chameleon-like quality which enables them to easily adapt to every personality and situation.

The Manipulator's Office Is Flexible

The office of a manipulator/facilitator does not reveal anything about its occupant. There are no diplomas, awards, or family photographs around. Even if the manipulator is married, he or she doesn't wear a wedding ring. Sophisticated office equipment and visible data are also missing. The office furniture is current but not plush or trendy, perhaps a slight cut above average. Nothing flashy. Modern art hangs from the walls which says absolutely nothing about the owner, but the visitor's opinion of it is solicited. There is probably a concealed wet bar, but if the visitor is a teetotaler, he or she would never know of its existence. Sometimes a round table is used for meetings so that differences in rank are not apparent. There is a conscious effort to downplay the trappings of power and influence, but you feel their subtle presence. It is both stimulating and and intimidating.

The Manipulator's Car Is Calculated Comfort

Depending upon who you are and what the manipulator/facilitator wants from you, this wily one would drive one of several kinds of cars in order to influence you.

If you are perceived as an	the manipulator/facilitator will drive a:
Achiever/technician	High-tech silver Volvo
Affiliator/pleaser	Light blue Ford Aerostar van or Jeep Cherokee
Power boss/commander	Black Cadillac
Avoider/abdicator	Light gray Oldsmobile
Manipulator/facilitator	White Mercedes-Benz

If the manipulator/facilitator owns only one automobile, it is probably a neutral-color Buick Electra or Oldsmobile 98.

Whoever you are, you will feel quite comfortable and very much at ease in the manipulator's car and thus can be more readily manipulated. If she or he feels that you can be intimidated, manipulator/facilitators will come on like Attila the Hun, but this type also knows how to mumble with the best of the avoiders. Usually the manipulator applies alternate doses of charm and logic to accomplish his or her interpersonal goals.

Manipulator/Facilitator Analysis

The quality of decision making of manipulator/facilitators is superior to that of the other four personality types, but the process may vary in length depending upon the needs of situations and the objectives of long-range game plans. Manipulators seldom make unpopular decisions, usually allowing subordinates to take the credit or blame, whichever the case might be. They use their excellent delegation skills to develop a cadre of submanagers who will effectively execute the leadership role long after they leave the organization.

Finally, manipulator/facilitator sales managers are splendid motivators. There is usually an upbeat atmosphere in their organizations. Even those astute mavericks who are aware that they are being used by their boss love it—because their personal and professional needs are being met. They often admire and emulate this type of leader as a role model from whom they can learn. Do you care if your boss is using you to get what he or she wants, if you are getting what you want? As long as it isn't illegal, immoral, or fattening—do it!

The Case for Benevolent Manipulation

A classic case of benevolent manipulation was Maestro Eugene Ormandy's 42-year tenure as music director of the Philadelphia Symphony Orchestra. His long-term objective was to produce exquisite sound from the musicians. Whenever the public attended a concert, heard a live broadcast, or listened to a recording of that ensemble, they were impressed by the world-famous "Philadelphia Sound."

Now, I would like to ask you: was this a positive or a negative goal? Were the players in that orchestra in 1980 the same musicians who were there in 1938, when Ormandy first assumed its leadership? Of course not, they all had either died or retired by that later date. Although the goal remained the same, and the leader remained at the helm, the players were all "used up" in the process. Do you think that they resented their roles, or do you think that they were proud to be a part of this internationally renowned orchestra? Obviously, Ormandy had created a long-term "win-win" situation for all members of his organization, as well as the discerning music public in general. Like the famous orchestra conductor, you, too, can orchestrate "win-win" situations for your mavericks, your firm, and its customers.

Psychological Profiling Summary: A Dual-Purpose Theory

Now that you've had a few hearty belly laughs at the expense of each of the five personality types, please keep these sobering thoughts in mind: As mentioned before, this material applies to the *manager* as well as the *managed*. In other words, these profiles can also describe yourself. It's a dual-purpose theory which will enable you to assess your own effectiveness in using the various sales management methods that we shall be analyzing in the following chapters.

Your mental attitude and experiences as a former maverick range rider will color your assessment and ability to implement each of these suggested techniques. They will also affect your effectiveness as a leader. So put your outlaw ways behind you, hang up your gun belt, and start getting the selling job done through other people—your mavericks.

One other important point before we saddle up and hit the dusty trail: Since I'm going to be referring frequently to each of the five personality types in subsequent chapters, I'm going to use some shorthand terms to avoid repetition of these rather syllable-laden types. Therefore, in addition to the numbers of the types introduced above, I will employ the following short forms:

1. affiliator/pleaser: A/P or affiliator

2. power boss/commander: PB/C or power boss

3. avoider/abdicator: A/A or avoider

4. achiever/technician: A/T or achiever

5. manipulator/facilitator: M/F or manipulator

Chapter 2 Roundup

You should use the psychological profiling of mavericks wisely because human beings are dynamic—they change and, like yourself, are constantly developing. By trait casting you can order the social field and obtain valuable insights into the personalities of your mavericks, customers, fellow managers, superiors, and even yourself. (Again, this matrix applies equally well to you as to your subordinates.) If you have correctly assessed the situation and carefully sized up the players, you can pretty much predict behaviors.

In the chapters which follow, you will see how you can use this human-skills knowledge to shape the behavior of your mavericks, understand how they perceive your leadership style, and learn how any of these five different personality types can become not only your best salesperson and most valuable customer but even President of the United States—the ultimate leadership position.

3

From Maverick to President: A Profiling Exercise

The only prize much cared for by the powerful is power. The prize of the general is not a bigger tent, but command.
OLIVER WENDELL HOLMES, JR.

Introduction to Presidential Profiling

Who rises to positions of power and influence in our society? Which one of the five personality types becomes the most powerful leader in the world—the President of the United States of America? Why are we picking on the Presidents? Don't they have enough worries and responsibilities as it is, without our poking around, looking for additional psychological insights? Certainly. But you need the profiling practice, and I can't think of a more visible target to which you could apply your new-found knowledge of personalities. So if you don't become political, emotional, or religious, we can find out who winds up in the White House most frequently. Besides, the President is, in a sense, the ultimate maverick.

Profiling of Presidents

Let's begin our psychological profiling of Presidents with Ronnie Reagan's idol, Calvin Coolidge, and then continue down through presidential history to the present incumbent at this writing, George Bush. While it's true that only a mere handful of them could ever qualify as genuine rawhide mavericks, their behavior while occupying the Oval Office will give you valuable clues for sizing up people both inside and outside your company so that you can manage their actions.

After you have analyzed each President in terms of his personality and power style, you may refer to Chap. 13 for the correct answers. It's appropriately entitled "The Sales Manager's Manual" and contains answers to this and other assignments which appear throughout this book. After all, if your mavericks can refer to their sales manuals when in doubt or trouble, why can't sales managers have a guide which they can consult? Who knows, it just might save your hide one day! Anyhow, if you can accurately size up the Presidents, perhaps you will do as well with the various personalities who influence your life and career progress. That's the bottom line of this profiling exercise.

John Calvin Coolidge (1923–1929)

Calvin Coolidge was a New England schoolteacher who became a compromise choice for the Vice Presidency. When Harding suddenly died in office, Coolidge became our thirtieth President.

Coolidge was isolationist and taciturn, believing that "the business of America is business." He gave new meaning to the term *laconic statement*. While attending a political convention, he was confronted by an eager reporter who had a hundred-dollar bet with his editor that he could get the shy President to say more than two words to him that evening. "You lose" was old Cal's laconic reply.

The National Archives in Washington, D.C., contains the comments made by each President regarding their finest accomplishments during their term in office. What do you think Coolidge said? "My best achievement as President of the United States was that I minded my own business." Which of the five personality types was President Coolidge?

Herbert Clark Hoover (1929–1933)

When Coolidge "did not choose to run" for a second term in the Oval Office, Herbert Hoover got the job. He was a superb mining engineer and a talented executive with awesome administrative skills and became a multimillionaire before embarking on a career of public service that would last over 40 years.

Hoover won world renown as administrator of food supplies during World War I, followed by eight highly successful years as Secretary of Commerce under both Harding and Coolidge. When the Great Depression began, he believed that federal intervention was a "dangerous thing" and that economic salvation could come only from the private sector. As things got worse he resisted outright relief to the millions of unemployed people, judging it to be "economically unsound" as well as "morally offensive, sapping the initiative of the working class."

The economy was "fundamentally sound," said Hoover, and would right itself if only the nation remained confident. But one of the biggest problems in restoring the nation's confidence was the President himself. Because he was a very private person, Hoover had neither the desire nor the ability to communicate with the public on a personal basis.

Although he felt that anarchy in the republic was intolerable and that poverty was a national disgrace, the Hoover administration did absolutely nothing to change the downward course of social and economic events. His inaction cost him a second term in office. What was his personality type?

Franklin Delano Roosevelt (1933–1945)

In many ways Franklin Roosevelt was not what he appeared to be. His patrician background provided him with social and financial credentials more common to the Republican party than to his own. Although crippled by polio from the waist down, most people did not know it. The only photographs or newsreel clips of the President showed him seated behind a desk or standing erect, supported by secret servicemen. His acceptance speech contained these words: "I pledge you, I pledge myself, to a new deal for the American people."

And thus the New Deal was born. Roosevelt had campaigned for a balanced federal budget and frugality in government spending—both of which he blatantly violated as President. The avalanche of legislation that marked his first year in the White House is well known, as is the declaration of a bank holiday, the calling in of gold, and the creation of an "alphabet soup" of new government agencies, including the FBI and the Social Security Act. Some special programs like the NRA, the CCC, etc., which were designed to put unemployed people back to work, were eventually struck down by the Supreme Court as unconstitutional.

An effective and charismatic speaker, FDR used his "fireside chats" to explain his actions to the public in simple terms. In those pretelevision days, he had the uncanny ability to articulate the sentiments of the people. He was so persuasive that he was elected to the Presidency four times, despite the two-term precedent which was set by George Washington. If Roosevelt hadn't died in office, he might have tried for a fifth term.

Before the United States became actively involved in World War II, Roosevelt endorsed the lend-lease program whereby the United States shipped arms to Great Britain in their struggle against Nazi Germany. He also approved General Claire Chennault's founding of the American Volunteer Group ("Flying Tigers"), who fought with the Nationalist Chinese against the Japanese long before the United States was at war with Japan.

It is still debated whether Roosevelt had advance knowledge that the Japanese were planning to bomb Pearl Harbor. The oil embargo on Japan and the freezing of Japanese assets in America brought about that attack on Pearl Harbor, which finally resolved public opinion to officially declare war. What kind of leader could orchestrate all of these diverse events so skillfully?

Harry S. Truman (1945–1953)

Like most strong leaders who surround themselves with weaklings in the number-two position, Roosevelt thought that this "plain-talking" man from Missouri was a pushover. Previously he had dropped Henry A. Wallace as his running mate because old Henry was getting too popular with the masses and was also involved with the American Communist movement.

When FDR suddenly died in office, however, Truman quickly asserted his strong leadership. He pulled no punches and always told it like it was. "The buck stops here" and "If you can't stand the heat, get out of the kitchen" were among his favorite sayings. No chief executive ever fell heir to such a tremendous burden on such short notice, but Truman proved to be decisive and logical. Among his most controversial decisions were the dropping of the atomic bomb on Japan, the firing of General Douglas MacArthur for insubordination, and quarreling with John L. Lewis, the powerful leader of the United Mine Workers.

Hiroshima and Nagasaki

The U.S. invasion of the Japanese mainland would cost x number of American lives, while dropping the bomb would cost y number of Japanese lives. Therefore, x times y equals "bombs away!"

General MacArthur and the Korean War

"Check the U.S. Constitution, Doug, and you will see that the Chief of *all* the armed forces is the President, not the generalissimo. Sayonara!"

John L. Lewis Wants to Be Vice President

Despite the fact that the American Labor Union movement put the Democratic Party into the White House during the 1930s and 1940s, Truman felt that Lewis was not qualified to be his running mate in 1948. The crusty UMW chief played hardball with Harry by calling a nationwide strike. The President responded by sending in the National Guard to man the coal mines. There is a famous photo of John L. Lewis seated on a chair being escorted out of a mine by two National Guardsmen.

Despite his volatility, President Truman listened to reason, read the data, and followed current trends and events most astutely. "Give-'em-hell-Harry" confounded the critics by winning the 1948 election from Thomas E. Dewey, the popular Governor of New York. His stormy tenure in office aptly illustrates situational leadership at its best. (According to this theory, the situation — or crisis — will produce the leader who is best qualified to handle the situation.) Now, who makes controversial decisions and backs them up with logic?

Dwight David Eisenhower
(1953–1961)

For many people, Dwight Eisenhower was an enigma. Do not be deceived by the PR campaign slogan for the 1952 election, "I like Ike"; he was certainly not an affiliator/pleaser. Let's examine his presidential record for some clues to his personality. Eight years in the Oval Office, and *nothing happened*. Oh yes, he did balance the budget and keep inflation to a minimum. Although minor miracles today, they were considered commonplace then.

If nothing happened, where was Ike? He was either playing golf with his military buddies or lying in the hospital with heart spasms. Rumor had it that it was really Sherman Adams, his chief of staff, who was running the country during the Eisenhower administration. So far, this sounds like a classic avoider/abdicator, who abdicates power to others rather than lead.

But let's not be too hasty in our assessment of Ike's personality. It might be instructive to change the leadership situation and see what we get. What was the leadership style of *General* Eisenhower, head of the Allied invasion of Europe during World War II? Who were his subordinate leaders? On his right was General George S. Patton, a maverick power boss/commander.

If Patton hadn't run out of petrol, he would probably be somewhere in Siberia by now. It's also no secret whom Patton felt was the *real* enemy — the country that got us into the war with Germany? England, of course. After the Germans were defeated and the Russians subdued, he wanted to turn right around and "mop up the British." Remember those infamous speeches that he made in England which nearly caused his fall from grace and power?

Now, if that weren't bad enough, who was on Eisenhower's left hand, heading up the British, Aussie, and South African troops? None other than the English maverick General Bernard Law (became first viscount) Montgomery. This power boss/commander was outspoken in his criticism of the American domination of the war effort and openly coveted Ike's leadership job. Now, who else but a _____ (you fill in the blank) could keep these two power boss subordinate officers from fighting *each other* rather than fighting the enemy? Apparently a change in leadership situation requires a different style of leadership. Which personality type has that kind of flexibility?

John Fitzgerald Kennedy
(1961–1963)

If charisma is a characteristic for leadership, then this charming man from Massachusetts had it in abundance. With his good looks, boyish smile, and witty sense of humor, Kennedy used people and things to get the job done.

Written off as a weakling by Nikita Khrushchev at their Vienna summit shortly after he ascended to the U.S. presidency, Kennedy later earned his place in history by his courageous stand during the Cuban missile crisis. Communist Cuba had been the site of Kennedy's greatest failure, during the Bay of Pigs invasion, and now was his greatest success.

He never had much of a legislative program, but he brought more people into public life than any other President in history. Kennedy was our first "television President" and the finest communicator in the White House since Franklin Roosevelt. Although he did not live long enough to reach his full presidential potential, JFK began the Peace Corps and the civil rights affirmative action programs. What type of personality was Kennedy?

Lyndon Baines Johnson
(1963–1969)

LBJ: What kind of personality has bold initials instead of a name? If you haven't figured out what Lyndon Johnson was by now, here are more clues. He was a rough and tough Texas maverick who did a great job, domesticwise. He got more legislation passed through Congress than any other President since FDR. But *how* did he do it? After cashing in on the sentiment regarding his predecessor's untimely death, he also knew which heads to knock together on Capitol Hill. During negotiations, "You owe me one!" was a favorite and effective expression.

The Vietnam War and his rivalry with Robert Kennedy hurt him. If you had four bars on your shoulder, he believed everything you said. This led to further involvement in an unpopular war. His public disdain for Robert Kennedy split the party and opened the door for Richard Nixon and the Republican Party.

Richard Milhous Nixon (1969–1974)

They don't call him "Tricky Dick" without good reason. Here was a manipulator who got caught in the act of manipulating. Pity. Nobody ever went into the White House better prepared. He was a lawyer, a member of Congress, and a member of the Senate and spent eight years as Vice President. You know that he had a great foreign policy record. The trouble with Nixon was that he had no faith, no trust, and he had a bad group around him. Thomas P. "Tip" O'Neill, House Speaker under eight Presidents, used to play poker with Nixon and said, "Any guy who would screech over losing 40 bucks shouldn't be President of the United States!"

Under every manipulator/facilitator is a power boss/commander to do the dirty work. Since a manipulator leader avoids making unpopular decisions, observe how Nixon related to H. R. Haldeman, his chief of domestic affairs, in this fictionalized dialogue:

> NIXON: "Hey, H. R., those kids at UCLA are raising hell again. What do *you* think we should do about it?"
>
> HALDEMAN: "I think that we should kill the bastards!"
>
> NIXON: "Well, if that's what *you* want to do…"

Naturally, Haldeman's people go out and beat up the kids. Since power bosses confuse action with achievement, they are always ready to jump into the fray. "Ready, fire, aim!" is their modus operandi. Notice here how well Nixon knew his man; whenever Nixon asked a question which appealed to his power boss subordinate's pugilistic nature, Nixon would get the desired response, namely beating up those college kids.

If beating up the kids was a popular thing to do—and public opinion favored it—who would get the credit for this valorous deed? Naturally, it would be Haldeman because he was up-front and visible during the entire violent proceeding. Nixon—the true instigator—did not have to

get the credit because he had delegated this assignment to a PB/C subordinate who craved recognition and loved to prove himself on these
types of challenges.

And what is the motivational impact on Haldeman? "Man, I've got
the greatest job in the world. I'm right there where the action is, doing
all those fun things like raising hell and kicking ass. That yo-yo in the
White House isn't doing a thing. I'm the one who is really running this
show."

Power bosses are so egocentric and insensitive that they can be standing at the front of a group, beating their chest (patting themselves on
the back or pounding their shoe on the podium), and proclaiming their
awesome powers while everyone else in the room knows that the real
boss is sitting quietly at the back of the room, taking notes. They can
easily be manipulated.

Now who would get the credit for beating up the kids if public opinion were indignant over such an abuse of governmental power? Naturally, it would be the same visible person. "Tricky Dick" had achieved
his objective and now this subordinate was expendable. Nixon would
appear before a national prime-time television audience, wearing his
"sincere" suit (without the hanger in it) and a very concerned demeanor.

> NIXON: "Mr. and Mrs. America. I am truly outraged that a member of my
> staff would carry on in such an irresponsible manner. Of course I ac-
> cepted his resignation. Wouldn't you?"

Manipulator/facilitators remain behind the scenes and are splendid
delegators. Since they are relatively ego-detached, these leaders do not
need recognition for the successful completion of their strategic plans.
They use up people and other available resources to attain their objectives, and are willing to lose every battle if they can win the war. Good
manipulators never get caught, Nixon did. Apparently his ego got in
the way.

Gerald Rudolph Ford (1974–1977)

Jerry Ford was the right man at the right time. When Nixon resigned,
the senator from Michigan succeeded to the presidency. Ford was popular with both sides of the political aisle. He wasn't in the White House
long enough to have any kind of substantial record, although it was a
transitional time. He tried to do the most popular things, like pardon-
ing Nixon and walking across a crowded room while chewing gum and

not bump into furniture or get hit by golf balls. When he ran unsuccessfully for President in his own right, Ford's campaign slogan was WIN—Whip Inflation Now.

Which personality type uses slogans and always tries to do popular things? If you get this one right, you will see that we now have at least one President who represents each of the five personality configurations. One of each flavor.

James Earl (Jimmy) Carter (1977–1981)

This peanut farmer was an engineer by training and detail-oriented by nature. They say that no one worked harder than Jimmy Carter in the White House, except Richard Nixon. Unfortunately he couldn't communicate very well and was very unpopular with the press. He also had a staff problem—very parochial.

Most of his decisions were controversial, and Carter either reversed himself or tried to use logic to explain them. Despite the Camp David accord—peace between Israel and Egypt—and other notable successes, the Iran hostage crisis did him in. Although a more decent man never sat in the White House, he was not reelected. Which type uses logic and makes controversial decisions?

Ronald Wilson Reagan (1981–1989)

No American President of the television age has combined the common touch with the unique ability to be everywhere at once in electronic form so successfully as Ronald Reagan. He was great with the media and had an appealing charisma. Many experts attribute his success in the Oval Office to his life as an actor. Every moment of every word was scripted, every place where Reagan was expected to stand was chalked with toe marks. The President was always being prepared for a performance and, after 45 years as an actor, usually knew his best camera angles. Some cynics define an actor as a body in search of a mind. "Who am I going to be today, Nancy? Check with your astrologer."

Nevertheless, both friend and foe admired the quality of leadership that he projected. Nobody in the history of America has ever had the affection that this man has had. In his speeches, Reagan quoted from both Democratic and Republican Presidents, utilizing the radio for his weekly broadcasts like Roosevelt before him. Anyone who could sell AWACs (Airborne Weapon and Control systems) to the Saudi Arabians and still retain Israel as a staunch ally has got to be a _____ (you fill in the personality style).

George Herbert Walker Bush
(1989–)

"Desert Storm" George is the first American President since Herbert Hoover for whom the presidency was his first elected political office. This former head of the CIA used to be known as the "invisible man." Who is George? Where has he been, and what does he stand for? These were the great unknowns until his leadership style began to emerge gradually during his first term in office.

Bush is a splendid delegator and usually avoids making unpopular decisions. He uses people and things to get the job done but frequently remains behind the scenes. James Baker, his Secretary of State, and other Cabinet members seem to get most of the credit and publicity for his administration's accomplishments.

Bush's low-key role behavior and his wimpy speaking voice lead some people to view him as an avoider/abdicator or a benign paternal figure at best. Neither perception is entirely accurate. He frequently changes roles and is definitely not what he appears to be.

Nevertheless, his masterly handling of the Persian Gulf crisis and his subsequent peace efforts in the Middle East ensured George Bush a place in history. How would you peg this sometimes invisible President?

Chapter 3 Roundup

In reviewing the psychological profiles of a dozen Presidents of the United States, did you see certain patterns of behavior emerge? Did you see similar personality traits and actions in your subordinates, fellow managers, superiors, and even customers? If so, you have taken a giant step forward in managing mavericks. The key to organizational development is understanding human behavior so that you can effectively manage the relationships of your subordinates in a mutually beneficial manner.

4

Completing the Transition

Experience is the name everyone gives to their mistakes.
OSCAR WILDE

Introduction to the Wild West of Sales Management

Most sales managers have been selling much longer than they have been managers, and like the Lone Ranger of western folklore, they are people of action who are used to getting the job done themselves. As a result, the transition from sales*person* to sales *executive* is a challenge. Some individuals never really make it.

Failure rates among new sales managers average from 25 to 30 percent. In some companies they are as high as 50 percent. When these leaders fail—or are ineffective—the cost to their firms is enormous, even ignoring the price of the wrecked careers of sales mavericks who might have succeeded if they had been adequately supervised by more competent managers. What about the loss to the company of the order productivity and leadership of these former star performers in the field?

In previous chapters, material was introduced on the leadership dimensions of sales management, which included delegation, essential skills and functions, role modeling, and the psychological profiling of mavericks. A case for benevolent manipulation was made as well as the fact that any of the five personality types could become your best salesperson, boss, customer, or even President of the United States. This chapter will pull all of these concepts together in order to help you complete your successful transition from selling to managing.

Analyzing Your Role as Sales Manager

In your previous job as sales associate, your main activities were directed toward developing accounts and sales volume. Now the game has changed and you must *develop salespeople* who will generate increasingly profitable sales revenue. You are responsible for achieving corporate sales volume objectives with and through your mavericks. Depending upon the type of industry that your company is in and whether you are selling a product or a service, you will probably divide your work week in a manner similar to the following:

Sales Management Activities

Selling	33%
Personnel	22%
Marketing	18%
Administration	20%
Finances	7%
Total	100%

How do these activities and their time allocations compare with the realities of your sales management situation? Should you make any changes?

In executing these duties and responsibilities, you must understand what managing is and what it is not. Most new sales managers have difficulty deciding which activities are *managing* and which ones are *nonmanaging* or *doing* roles. It is one of the many reasons for failure on the job as they wind up doing more than they should, and managing less than is required.

The following true-life case study demonstrates how effective salespersons can become ineffective sales managers because of their inability to distinguish between doing and managing. After you have analyzed this case study, you should try your luck with the twenty-question self-quiz at the end of this chapter.

Case Study

The Case of the Newly Appointed Sales Manager

As soon as Tom Greene became manager of the Chicago branch office, he immediately held a meeting with his staff.

"I want this office to become the top branch office in the company within the next six months, or heads will roll." He then recounted some of his own sensational selling tactics as guidelines to be emulated.

"I am looking for maximum efforts. As you know, a salesperson's job is to sell, and if you can't produce orders up to my high standards, you might as well turn in your sales kits right now. You've got to either shape up or ship out. Understand?"

During the course of the meeting Greene seemed to detect some resentment from Harvey Blue, the office's most senior salesperson, who had also acted as interim branch manager. He suspected that Blue had wanted the promotion to branch manager and was disgruntled because he didn't get it. Greene decided to wait before he talked to him, believing that a hefty commission check would improve Blue's attitude.

Greene concluded the meeting with the announcement of an impromptu sales contest in which the top sales performer would win a trip to Las Vegas. The only goal that he set was to "beat the Detroit office," which was the top branch in the Midwestern Region. Greene reasoned that this contest would be a much needed "shot in the arm" for the sales staff plus an added "reward" to Blue, who was certain to win.

To set the pace for his sales team, Greene started to work his usual 60-hour week. Almost immediately, his salespeople proceeded to close new business at a rapid rate. The contest, coupled with Greene's long hours, caused some furious sales activity. As a result, Greene was rarely in the office. His dislike for paperwork put him consistently behind in submitting reports to the home office. He also did not press his staff for their required reports, with the result that many important administrative matters were completely ignored. He also decided that, because the main problem was immediate revenue, he and his staff would only call on new prospects and avoid all calls that were not sales connected. To him, courtesy and "problem" visits were a nuisance, and only in rare instances did he let his sales associates take time to "mend fences." Greene only asked his beleaguered subordinates one curt question: *"Where's the orders?"* He also reminded them that there was, on average, only a 19-inch difference between a pat on the back and a kick in the butt.

Greene's first major personnel problem was Loretta Holiday, a veteran salesperson with a consistently low sales record. The prior branch manager had once put Holiday on probation for taking too many holidays during the regular work week. Greene read Holiday's personnel file and concluded that she was a loser and had no business being in sales. A few days later, a friend of Greene's wife said that she had seen Holiday playing golf at a nearby country club one afternoon when she should have been out there selling in the field like the rest of the reps. Greene was so incensed that he called Holiday into his office and fired her right on the spot. An immediate replacement had to be found.

A few weeks later, Greene hired Howard LaFlash, following a

brief interview and a glowing recommendation from a local
headhunter. LaFlash had briefly worked in Dallas as a Bible
salesman and had also sold for half a dozen competitive firms in the
Southwest during the past five years.

There was another surge of new orders, but there also seemed to
be a sharp increase in the number and intensity of customer
complaints. The home office became concerned and asked Greene
to personally call on every problem account and report his findings.
The new branch manager dropped everything else and completed
this assignment in a short period of time. "No need to be alarmed,"
he assured the home office. "The problem is one of our well-known
problem accounts, All American Antics. Ever since they expanded
their operations they think that they can push their suppliers
around. They are up to their usual antics, stirring things up in the
territory. Those bums give our competitors the same bad time.
Don't sweat it, I'll handle that account personally. I know how to
ride a tiger."

Shortly afterwards, Greene held a sales meeting for his entire
staff, including his technical support team. He started out by
awarding the Las Vegas trip to Blue, who won the sales contest by a
wide margin. He also criticized the rest of his salespeople for
"dragging their feet" and letting him down. He pointed out that
prospecting had fallen off and reminded them that there was no
place for loafers in his outfit. He cited Loretta Holiday's abrupt
dismissal as an example which he would not hesitate to follow with
any of them.

His salespeople complained that problem accounts were cutting
into their selling time and that some customer complaints required
almost a full week to resolve. Greene assured them that he would
hire another customer service rep soon to ease the work load. A
phone call cut that meeting short.

The following week, Greene received some disconcerting news.
Cyco Products was canceling their account because of unacceptable
programming and technical support for a new systems application.
Greene was caught completely by surprise. He reviewed the call
reports on Cyco Products and found them hopelessly out of date.
He recalled that his first and only sales call on this large customer
was very pleasant and everyone seemed happy.

Greene saw red, called in his entire technical support staff, and
chewed them out thoroughly. He told them to fix it or he would
find some other "eggheads" who would. The next day after his
temper tantrum, one technical assistant quit. Another asked to be
transferred to Alaska.

Greene called the home office and asked for a support team "with
guts" to be sent immediately to Chicago. Before the new group
arrived, Horace Snodgrass, the technical support manager,
convinced Greene that the difficulty with Cyco Products was only a
misunderstanding over contract specifications, not a technical
deficiency in their product. Snodgrass stated that he had written a

memo to Greene several weeks earlier which explained the problem. Greene and Snodgrass resolved the matter simply by making a joint call on Cyco Products and clarifying several ambiguous terms to Cyco's satisfaction.

Case Conclusion

Greene decided to increase his work hours because his problems were mounting and he was running out of time. He was

1. Trying to recruit another customer service rep
2. Making sales calls alone or with struggling members of his staff
3. Trying to cope with his increased paperwork
4. Endeavoring to devote more time to his administrative people, who seemed inundated with a variety of accounting, procedural, and personnel problems

In addition, he was having his own "people problems" too. One of his best sales associates was not making quota; another one — transferred from the technical staff — was slow getting started and might not make it. Harvey Blue was brooding over something or other and showing signs of unrest, while Howard LaFlash was an outright dud. His initial burst of steam had fizzled, and he was working well below expectations — a real flash-in-the-pan. Furthermore, Greene's rapport with Horace Snodgrass had deteriorated as a result of the Cyco Products affair and his own hot-tempered accusations.

Greene's Solution Was Simple

Although Tom Greene concluded that the only solution to all these problems was to hire more people just like himself, you may wish to make other recommendations.

- What are the key issues involved in this case?
- What did Greene do wrong?
- What would you have done differently?
- What are the personality profiles of each individual?

Case Study Analysis

This case study illustrates a super salesperson's inability to make the transition from selling to managing. Tom Greene was a forceful *doer* who did not practice the basic principles of sales management.

If *management* is defined as getting work done through other people, then your task as sales manager is to mold a group of independent-minded mavericks into a cohesive sales team. Salespeople are completely unlike any other employees; they value their freedom of action and frequently break the rules. Your effective utilization of the following five principles of sales management will help you avoid Tom Greene's mistakes and ensure your tenure in office beyond the four-year barrier.

Principles of Sales Management

Planning

Planning is a technical skill which is part of the administrative side of sales management. It is your prime responsibility. It consists of setting objectives and determining what needs to be done by whom, by when, and with what resources in order to fulfill your assigned duties and responsibilities. In most firms, long-range planning starts with a sales forecast, which is made after careful consideration of such factors as current economic conditions, trends in your industry, the nature and number of your competitors, and probable demand for new products, services, and technologies.

General Eisenhower once said that "plans are nothing, but *planning* is everything." Planning is not possible, however, until a job situation analysis is performed. Therefore, you should begin with a position analysis—what senior management expects of you. Performance is impossible without a clear understanding of the specific job functions that you will be held responsible for and how your boss perceives their relative importance. The best guides are your position title and job description, which usually contains a list of general duties and responsibilities that go with the position title.

Job descriptions frequently describe the general duties and responsibilities of the person who held the position when the form was last revised. Unless the job description has been written within the last year, it is probably outdated and bears little resemblance to your present sales management position. What is even more important is that you and your boss agree on the values and priorities of your job. A clear understanding of the specific functions and responsibilities of your position and how you will be evaluated on your performance is crucial to your success on the job. It is possible that you and your boss have different views on the priorities of your position.

The planning steps after the situation analysis include:

- Establishing objectives
- Developing strategies

- Budgeting
- Developing action plans
- Establishing controls

You will want to be flexible enough to be able to test the feasibility of implementing your plans while there is still time to take remedial action. Sales manager personality types differ in their approaches to, and appreciation of, planning. Achiever/technicians, manipulator/facilitators, and avoider/abdicators are excellent planners, whereas power boss/commanders usually proceed on instinct and gut feel. Affiliator/pleasers would rather "wing it" and hope for the best.

Organizing

Organizing all of your available resources in working order is the second sales management principle. You will be deeply involved with the number and kinds of positions in your organization, along with their corresponding duties and responsibilities required to attain or exceed objectives. You will be called upon to provide input as to what will be the most effective organization to produce maximum sales volume and profits for your firm and optimal satisfaction for your customers.

Some of the more important factors are the allocation of resources, territory alignments, budgetary considerations, and administrative requirements. Achiever/technicians and manipulator/facilitators are the best-organized executives. Depending on their mood, avoider/abdicators can either be very good or extremely disorganized. Some like to have "a place for everything and everything in its place," while others are as sloppy as they come. Power boss/commanders couldn't care less, while an affiliator/pleaser is out to lunch on this one ("Next year we're going to get organized.").

Staffing

Recruiting, selecting, and hiring successful mavericks is next in the sequence of sales management principles, but foremost in importance. *Recruitment should be a continuous process, not one indulged in only when a vacancy occurs.* A proactive approach to recruiting reduces the likelihood of holding on to a salesperson whom you should let go or hiring an unqualified maverick because you have an open territory. Isn't this exactly what Tom Greene did to himself in the case study when he impulsively fired Loretta Holiday and was compelled to hire Howard LaFlash, the ex-Bible salesman, because he now had an open territory?

Prior to initiating *any* recruitment program, you must determine your organizational requirements as well as the caliber and experience level of your sales force. Will it be composed of full-time company sales personnel, manufacturer's reps, distributors, or some combination thereof?

Guidelines for utilizing full-time company salespeople are budget considerations, market requirements, the nature of your customers and product line, the competition, company image considerations, and your industry customs and traditions.

Manufacturer's reps are used by both large and small firms who have a limited number of products, are short on funds, or want to reduce their cashflow strain. Sometimes a rep firm is used when a firm introduces a new product line that is completely foreign to their existing sales force or it wants to enter a new geographic market that is not developed enough to support a full-time company salesperson.

Staffing is the favorite function of the affiliator/pleaser sales manager. He or she considers it an important social function and the opportunity to meet many new and exciting people. Unfortunately they do a poor job because they "love" everybody who walks into their offices. Achiever/technicians consider staffing a necessary evil ("Don't we have the technology to do it without salespeople?") but usually do an excellent job. Avoider/abdicators somehow never get around to doing it. They would just as soon abdicate this job responsibility completely if they could. Meeting new people can be a painful experience, and then you have to decide which one of those braggarts will be able to sell. When they finally do get involved in the recruitment process, they have trouble making decisions.

Power boss/commanders don't have much time for such "trivial" tasks, although they don't mind impressing sales applicants with their selling and sales management prowess. Relying on intuition, however, they somehow do a better than average job. Manipulator/facilitators do the best job of all and have great success in *retaining* their mavericks.

Retention is the name of the game on the wild western frontier of sales management, where folks are buying *relationships* more than products, services, or systems. Source credibility and continuity of service by the same mavericks, year in and year out, builds customer confidence and market share. Without a stable sales force, you cannot ever hope to maintain your customer base or your market position over the long run. Some sales manager personality types are better than others at retaining their salespeople, but it is an ability well worth cultivating. Keep that in mind whenever you get the urge to fire a maverick sales superstar because he or she wanted to do the job their way, rather than your way. It would be like cutting off your nose to spite your face.

After these staffing considerations have been resolved and the necessary recruitment funds have been allocated, your next step is to develop strategies for identifying prospective sales candidates and then build a pool of available recruits on an ongoing basis. Subsequent chapters will cover the selection process and techniques for retaining your mavericks — your most valuable assets.

Directing

Directing means exercising leadership and adroit human skills in implementing your plans through other people in order to reach or exceed your job objectives. This task requires exceptional skills in delegation, interpersonal communication, and motivation. Equally important are training, coaching, and counseling.

You must coordinate all of your mavericks' activities and see that they are carried out in relation to their importance and with a minimum of conflict. The team concept of selling must take precedence over individual initiative. The group attitude must be "all for one and one for all," because successful sales teams are built on cooperation and interdependence. Sometimes this coordination of effort is difficult because of the geographic dispersion of your salespeople and the extensive travel that is required of them and you. Nevertheless, it must be done, and you will be held accountable by your boss for your ability to do so on a consistent basis.

Power boss/commander sales managers don't direct, they command. Although poor motivators, they can obtain superb results in the short run because of their forceful leadership style. They are good at bossing other people around and know how to get things moving. Achiever/technicians and manipulator/facilitators draw upon the diverse talents of their mavericks to get concerted action, although achiever sales managers tend to be somewhat myopic and detached. Manipulator sales managers orchestrate win-win situations that challenge and motivate their sales team members. Avoider/abdicators tend to linger in the background, often relying on company policies and procedures as guidelines for group action. Affiliator/pleasers view their role as cheerleader and pacifier. They are excellent at building group relationships, "keeping the peace," and building esprit de corps.

Controlling

Controlling your organizational environment is the hallmark of every effective sales executive. When managing mavericks, it is your most formidable challenge. In the planning phase you set departmental objectives and established what constituted satisfactory performance and what could go wrong along the way. In other words, you set standards for each major step in your game plan so that you can measure performance and be able to make any appropriate changes when necessary.

Exert control over your mavericks to ensure that the work that you and they perform achieves the step-by-step results for which you planned. Although more easily said than done, this is a structured way of making sure that goals are attained; it also provides timely visibility with a minimum expenditure of time and effort. Then your standards or indicators will enable you to gauge effective performance and know later that you are proceeding satisfactorily toward your goals.

Measuring Performance

Performance measurement is the process of ascertaining what actually happened as compared with what was planned. The indicators you examine should reveal if certain areas of performance are inadequate. The information you need can be gleaned from personal observations, meetings, your call report system, telephone contacts, and customer feedback. To make certain that you are on target, or need to get back on track, you should measure performance frequently and regularly— daily, monthly, or at whatever interval you feel is best. Keep your options open and be prepared to take corrective action or establish alternative action plans.

Controls are needed to ensure profitability as well as measuring progress toward goals. The reports that you are required to prepare on a weekly, monthly, or quarterly basis are each designed to facilitate this sales management process by providing you and your boss with the information needed to set or update objectives, plan effective strategies, and control your mavericks to be certain that organizational objectives are reached. Effective strategy is based on sound planning, accurate market intelligence, and flexible control mechanisms.

Your company's policies may enhance or inhibit your ability to control all of the activities in your department. They dictate the format of performance records and administrative procedures. Your challenge is to minimize the time spent in administrative functions and controlling activities so you can maximize the time spent out in the field developing your salespeople. Your most productive time will be invested in the field, monitoring performance, motivating, and developing your mavericks. You can avoid administrative traps by having clear-cut objectives and by keeping your priorities straight.

Each sales manager personality type, however, has divergent views on the controlling function. PB/Cs run a "tight ship" and are big on controls—their control. It's their strong suit. A/Ts, M/Fs, and A/As are all excellent in establishing the applicable control mechanisms, but only the manipulators implement them in a flexible and creative manner. They facilitate the attainment of their organizational goals by manipulating their mavericks and controlling their environment on a long-term, mutually beneficial basis. The free-spirited A/Ps don't believe in controls of *any* kind and would rather rely on their feelings and hunches. Who do you think has the best track record in this functional area?

Chapter 4 Roundup

Making the transition from selling to managing is a formidable challenge, requiring prior field selling experience and superb administrative skills. You are no longer the Lone Ranger; you are a manager and not a doer. Whatever got you into sales management is no longer good enough to keep you there. You must develop your mavericks into productive salespeople, just as you formerly developed your sales prospects into profitable accounts.

The effective application of the five basic principles of sales management—planning, organizing, staffing, directing, and controlling—will enable you to successfully complete the transition from selling to managing. They will also enhance your chances for success in this most demanding executive position. Depending upon your psychological personality profile, you will experience varying degrees of frustration as you endeavor to master each of these vital functions.

Doing versus Managing Self-Quiz

This self-probe will enable you to test your knowledge of the differences between managing and nonmanaging (doing) activities. The following 20 activities fall into one of these categories. You are to indicate whether they are managing or doing activities. The correct answers and their rationale can be found in Chap. 13, "The Sales Manager's Manual."

1. Calling on an account with one of your mavericks to show a customer that your company's management is interested in their business.

Managing ____ Doing ____

2. Making a sales presentation to a prospective customer to show one of your salespeople how to do it.

Managing ____ Doing ____

3. Making an independent call on an officer of a large account to cement customer relationships and promote additional business.

Managing ____ Doing ____

4. Explaining how to solve a work problem that one of your sales staff has just brought to you.

Managing ____ Doing ____

5. Filling out a form to recommend a salary increase for a member of your department.

Managing ____ Doing ____

6. Explaining to one of your mavericks why he or she is receiving a salary increase.

Managing ____ Doing ____

7. Interviewing a prospective salesperson who was referred to you by an employment agency.

Managing ____ Doing ____

8. Giving a telephone report of progress to your superior.

Managing ____ Doing ____

9. Asking one of your mavericks what they think about a selling idea that you have.

Managing ____ Doing ____

10. Planning and deciding on a dollar sales volume objective by each account.

Managing _____ Doing _____

11. Deciding what the cost budget request shall be for your sales office.

Managing _____ Doing _____

12. Reviewing monthly sales reports to determine progress toward specific sales volume objectives.

Managing _____ Doing _____

13. Deciding whether to meet a competitive price based upon considerations unknown to your maverick.

Managing _____ Doing _____

14. Deciding whether to recommend adding a position.

Managing _____ Doing _____

15. Drafting an improved office layout for your sales department.

Managing _____ Doing _____

16. Asking your mavericks to establish tentative six-month objectives for the number of personal calls to be made on targeted accounts.

Managing _____ Doing _____

17. Giving a speech about your firm's progress and plans to a local service club.

Managing _____ Doing _____

18. Transferring an account from Salesperson *A* to Salesperson *B* because Salesperson *A* did not devote the necessary time and effort to develop that account.

Managing _____ Doing _____

19. Phoning a plant manager to request help in solving a customer delivery problem for one of your mavericks.

Managing _____ Doing _____

20. Planning the extent to which your sales associates should use staff services during the next year in order to accomplish overall sales goals.

Managing _____ Doing _____

PART 2

How to Recruit, Select, and Hire Winners

I only hire salespeople who are in their thirties, married with three or more children, and carrying mortgages as big as the federal deficit. If they are up to their ears in debt, they'll need me more than I'll need them.

ANONYMOUS SALES MANAGER

5
Preinterviewing Activities That Pay Off

Natural Selection means Survival of the Fittest.   CHARLES ROBERT DARWIN

Introduction to Recruiting

This chapter helps you apply Darwin's theory to the selection of the maverick species of salesperson, where survival of the fittest is the name of the game. Your hiring activities will go through a natural selection process whereby you hope that a super salesperson, and not an ape, will emerge. You've probably got enough of those critters in your sales force already! Get ready, the great cattle call is on.

Selecting and retaining above-average order producers are two of the biggest challenges that you will ever face in sales management. To begin with, the costs can be staggering. It is estimated that investment in hiring and training of a new sales hand can range between $10,000 and $80,000 in direct expenses during the employee's first full year on the job. This price tag does not include business lost by inept mavericks or the higher cost of employee turnover. A sound recruiting system will enable you to reduce these astonishing costs while ensuring vigorous self-renewing sales success in your organization. We will discuss the preinterviewing or planning aspects along

---

Preinterviewing Activities Guidelines

1. Analyze selling job requirements.
2. Define successful job performance.
3. Establish job specifications.
   - Prepare a detailed job description.
   - Determine numerical requirements, such as sales quota, number of client calls, new accounts, trade-show attendance, and administrative duties.
4. Develop interview questions.
   - Current industry practices.
   - Your specific requirements.
   - Governmental guidelines, such as, Office of Federal Contract Compliance programs, Equal Employment Opportunity Commission, Civil Service Commission, and local state and municipal regulations.
5. Recruit a sufficient number of applicants.
6. Screen out unqualified job candidates.

Figure 5-1

with how each sales manager personality type copes with these diverse activities. See Fig. 5-1 for a summary.

Objectives of Planned Recruiting and Selection

The goals of a planned recruiting and selection program are to upgrade the quality level and order productivity of your mavericks, suppress turnover to an absolute minimum, recruit candidates with the qualifications needed for success in selling, screen out misfits, reduce lost time due to open territories, and finally, to take the guesswork out of the maverick selection process.

The Astronomical Cost of Sales Staff Turnover

Although there are many factors which influence sales force turnover, the most obvious reason is that the wrong rascal was hired to do the job in the first place. Most sales managers are lucky if they don't lose 50 percent of their newly hired mavericks within the first two years. Other devastating factors include:

Personality conflicts

Lack of sufficient training

Ineffective supervision

Raiding by unscrupulous competitors

Limited opportunities for advancement

A faulty compensation plan

A change in company ownership or its competitive position

It is much easier and far less costly to hire well-qualified and self-motivated individuals rather than to try to train and motivate mediocre mavericks who were mistakenly hired or inherited from your predecessor. Accurately assess the suitability of your applicants *before* investing in their selling potential. Recognize the selection process for what it really is — a good old-fashioned cattle auction. You are involved in buying one of the most costly animals on the range — human mavericks — and your judgment will constantly be on the line.

Expensive at Any Cost

To arrive at an accurate figure for the annual turnover cost for your firm, you should combine the total investment in recruiting, hiring, and training a new sales associate. Orders lost and business potential unrealized during the time that a territory is open or in transition should also be added to this figure. Then multiply this amount by the number of new salespeople hired during the year to replace those bodies lost as a result of turnover. Don't forget to include your own personal interviewing, training, and coaching time as well as relocation and sample equipment costs into your calculations. Analyzing each cost factor in this manner will prevent you from dealing with only the tip of the turnover iceberg and give you an idea of the magnitude of the problem that you are up against. It's a costly cattle drive, no matter how you look at it.

Determine Your Territory Requirements and Staff Qualifications

Depending on the type of position you are trying to fill, the nature of your industry, and the current economic situation, you may wish to con-

---

Checklist for Qualifying an Independent Rep Organization

Answers to the following questions will enable you to evaluate the qualifications of independent rep sales organizations whom you are considering to handle your product line in a specific territory.

1. Is this rep organization soundly financed?
2. How long have they been in business?
3. Do they show a consistent pattern of sales growth?
4. Do they cover your market area completely?
5. Is their office located conveniently to important customers? Are the premises neat and clean?
6. How stable is their partnership relationship?
7. Do they have a good reputation with your customers and those who influence their buying?
8. Do they have sufficient sales coverage? Are their salespeople under- or overqualified?
9. Do they have competent inside sales support personnel? How are they paid?
10. How many product lines do they carry? Which ones? (Competitive product lines are red flags.)
11. Do they maintain and use a mailing list?
12. To which professional organizations do they belong?
13. If they have to carry inventory, do they have suitable warehouse space? Is it convenient to freight carriers, and do they have adequate shipping and billing facilities?
14. Are they the kind of selling organization which would reflect favorably on your company?
15. Are the principals actively involved in the business? Are they planning to stay in business for a number of years into the future, or will one or more of them retire soon?

If the organization you're considering can pass this 15-point checklist with flying colors, you've got yourself a winner.

Figure 5-2

---

sider hiring an independent rep organization instead of one or more employees. See Fig. 5-2 for guidelines in qualifying these firms.

On the other hand, if it's the ideal sales rep that you are trying to lasso, you'll want to also consider your firm's projected growth and marketing strategies, your own annual sales forecast, and current competitive conditions in each of your sales territories. These are guidelines in deciding how many mavericks you will need and when. Your firm's personnel policies and available budget and the present job market conditions will establish pay ranges. Decide what you want, how many warm bodies you need, what it's going to cost to get them, and whether it's going to be worth it. Money alone won't do the job, as George Steinbrenner found out. When he owned the New York Yankees, this volatile maverick put together the best baseball team that money could buy, but they still failed to win the pennant. By the same token, you've got to forge a sales team which can consistently bring home the bacon.

Define Successful Job Performance

Contrary to popular western folklore, a good maverick *cannot* sell anything to anybody. He or she must have specific qualifications, training, and experience in order to do an acceptable job for you. But here's the rub. Do you know what is acceptable performance? Can you define it? Do you know exactly what you want in a salesperson or the kind of individual you are looking for? Which kind of personality types succeed in selling in your particular industry? What are their behavioral characteristics and patterns? These are some of the important questions that you should answer *before* you start placing any want ads. As you can see, there's no room for guesswork out on the recruiting range.

Determine the technical requirements (*can do*) of the sales job, motivational factors (*will do*), and the interpersonal and environmental factors (*fit*) for each particular territory. *Can Do* factors relate to your job candidate's ability to do the job. What specific experience, skills, technical knowledge, abilities, prior training, education, etc., are required or desired for successful sales performance? Not all "achievers" can achieve for you.

Will Do factors concern an applicant's desire to do the selling job. The question before you is "What specific behaviors are required or desired in order to be certain that he or she *will* work hard and behave in a manner which reflects positively on my company and is consistent with established success patterns?" This is a very real concern with maverick salespeople, who tend to be quite independent and ignore company rules and regulations if these get in their way.

Fit factors apply to corporate cultures and sales team building. The questions here are "Will this newcomer fit in with the present environmental circumstances of my sales job? Will he or she mesh well with the personalities of my current customers, fellow sales associates, and sales support staff? What is her or his psychological personality style? In short, *is he or she our kind of maverick?*" These three criteria, can do, will do, and fit, will enable you to establish the "knockout factors" for your available sales positions.

Keeping these three criteria in mind, complete your *job analysis* with the following sequential steps:

1. List the most important duties and responsibilities of this position. They are the foundation of your job description for this sales job.
2. Describe key involvement with others, such as clients, superiors, subordinates, peers, or other company contacts.
3. What are the potential sources of job satisfaction? Are there any systems or obstacles which might get in the way of performance?
4. What are the potential sources of dissatisfaction and/or demotivation? Information from termination interviews, the company "grapevine," and your industry network could provide important insights.
5. What job opportunities or career paths might be available within your company?

From this information, a realistic job description can be developed for each position in your sales organization. Examples of current job descriptions can be found in Chap. 13.

Your firm's human resources department can make an invaluable contribution as you define your requirements and search for candidates. This is their professional specialty. These executives can save you precious time by initially screening applicants; they can also protect you from the many legal pitfalls which beset the selection process. For example, if your firm's application form is more than five years old, it might be obsolete and request information that would violate a prospective employee's rights. This could set you up—as an agent of your employer—for a serious job discrimination lawsuit. The burden of proof rests on the employer, and current court decisions tend to favor the "little guy" over the big bad corporation. So don't overlook the resources of your human resources department.

However, if you are by nature a power boss/commander or an achiever/technician sales manager, you will brook no interference from anyone in "Human Resources." Typical comments are:

"After all, what do *they* know about selling and salespeople?"

"Most of them were raised on prunes and proverbs, and wouldn't know the difference between a steer and a stallion."

"They're all gurgle and no guts."

Avoider/abdicator, affiliator/pleaser, and manipulator/facilitator sales managers welcome all the help that they can get in this administrative area, but each for different reasons. The avoider is afraid to give up this task, fearing that his or her boss will think that she or he doesn't have any work to do but is also afraid to make any waves by refusing outside help. Affiliators are relieved to have someone else do the tedious paperwork and know that they aren't particularly good at it. Manipulator/facilitators view this involvement with other departments as a golden opportunity to size up their executives and develop interdepartmental rapport, thereby enhancing their career progress within the company.

Establish Job Specifications

Now that you know exactly what you are looking for in a new salesperson and have committed these requirements to paper, you will want to assemble them into a workable form. After defining the can do, will do, and fit factors, you are now ready to design your Job Specifications Worksheet for a Salesperson for use during your forthcoming employment interviews. Worksheet criteria are listed in Fig. 5-3.

The objective of your job specifications worksheet is to answer this key question: What is the best combination of these technical and nontechnical characteristics that will produce the highest level of achievement on the job? This is what you will be looking for during your employment interviews.

In your experience, which is easier to teach a new maverick — technical product knowledge or interpersonal selling skills? Your company culture and policy might favor one over the other and thus limit your hiring options. Your own personality style and bias are also subtle factors. For example, if you are an achiever/technician or an avoider/abdicator, you will emphasize technical factors. You will emphasize nontechnical factors if you are more emotional like the affiliator/pleasers or power boss/commanders. Manipulator/facilitators will opt for the best of both worlds. What are *you* looking for?

Recruitment Sources

Once you have determined the need for additional salespeople, obtained the necessary hiring budget, and drawn up a job description for the ideal candidate, you must know where to look for this talent. It's

---

Job Specifications Worksheet for a Salesperson

Technical Characteristics

1. *Selling experience.* Is it general or industry-specific? Does he or she know anything about my firm's type of product or service? How much range-rambling experience has the candidate had?
2. *Educational background.* Is a college degree required? If so, what kind of degree does this person have, and what was his or her class standing?
3. *Skill requirements.* Are technical, human, or conceptual skills needed? How much of the job requires mechanical, electrical, and high-tech skills as opposed to persuasive, communication, and leadership skills?

Nontechnical Characteristics

1. *Work habits.* Study the applicant's ambition, goals, and values. Notice his or her energy level, physical fitness, and appearance as well as signs of independence, creativity, and imagination. Does he or she have a technical or a relationship orientation?
2. *Occupational interests and objectives.* Discuss potential career paths. What are his or her other preferences, dislikes, and aptitudes?
3. *Intellectual functioning.* Is she or he "street smart" or long on theory? Look for flexibility and resourcefulness, thought-process agility, decision-making ability, as well as insight and depth of thinking.
4. *Emotional adjustment.* Notice the applicant's levels of maturity, stability, and reality orientation. What is his or her tolerance for criticism, desire for self-improvement, and overall success pattern? What is the candidate's self-image?

Figure 5-3

roundup time at the OK Corral, and you want to lasso the best mavericks for your outfit. Where are the best sources for these range riders?

Any experienced cowpoke will tell you that the most productive recruiting sources for sales reps are referrals from your best customers, loyal employees, personal acquaintances, business contacts, and professional association memberships, like Sales and Marketing Executives. This is your sales "network," and it also includes college and university placement offices as well as marketing professors who teach selling and sales management courses.

Employees from other departments in your firm can be developed into productive sales associates because of their current company background, same-industry experience, product knowledge, and active interest in selling. The same holds true for applicants who solicit you for a job or competitive salespeople who want to defect to your organization. Other good sources include trade shows, newspaper ads, and employment agencies.

How to Recruit Sufficient Numbers of Candidates

Always keep the "pipelines" open. A proactive approach to recruiting will ensure an adequate pool of talent that you can draw upon whenever the need arises. It's easier to get good salespeople when times are good and your mavericks are earning the big bucks. Spirits are high on the range, and the office has an upbeat atmosphere. Working for your firm seems very attractive, even to competitive reps whom you might covet.

When times are bad, or territories suddenly become open because of terminations, retirements, or transfers, you needn't panic because you have hopeful range hands sitting on the bench back at the ranch. Continuous recruiting means developing a reserve or pool of qualified prospects, some of whom might be currently employed by other firms but are willing to wait until an opening in your company occurs. That's how to keep the old maverick recruiting trough from drying up.

Always talk about your business and its fabulous selling opportunities at social functions and other occasions. Some sales managers even teach a university extension course in professional selling so that they can spot students with promising selling potential before a competitor does. Wherever you are and whatever you are doing, always be in a recruitment mode. It will pay off.

Techniques for Screening Out Unqualified Candidates

How do you keep the flakes and other misfits from infiltrating your sales organization? For starters, take a tip from this feisty sales manager who wanted to hire another telemarketer for her boiler-room operation. She placed an ad in a local newspaper with this tag line: "Respond by telephone or résumé." She screened out all of the applicants who sent résumés and only interviewed those candidates who were alert enough to respond by telephone. "Their job is to sell over the phone, not to write love letters. They must use that medium to sell themselves to me first. I'm their first big sale. If I don't like their telephone personality, why should my clientele?"

If telemarketing isn't one of your major job requirements, you will rely on résumés and completed job application forms to determine whom you will interview. If you receive a large number of résumés to review, you could delegate this time-consuming assignment to your secretary, an able assistant, or one of your senior mavericks. It saves you time and energy and is a learning experience for your subordinates. Some firms utilize the expert services of their human resources departments. The idea is to eliminate as many unqualified applicants as possible in a timely fashion and thereby make your eyeball-to-eyeball interviewing time more productive.

Conventional Screening Techniques

As soon as you have a sufficient number of job hopefuls, you can screen out those who are obviously unqualified by measuring them against the following criteria:

- *Earnings.*   Is he or she presently making about what your firm could pay or more, requiring this individual to accept a lateral move or a cut in pay? If either is true, the candidate probably won't last very long.

- *Location.*   Is he or she currently living too far away to justify your firm's paying moving expenses until you have eliminated all closer candidates? Also, real estate prices might be so prohibitive in the sales territory that applicants from other regions might be reluctant to accept your offer, no matter how lucrative it is.

- *Experience.*   Is the quantity or quality of the applicant's experience insufficient or too much for the job? Are they under- or overqualified? If either is the case, he or she will soon be history.

- *Telephone impressions.*   Conduct a preliminary screening interview over the phone. Find out what your applicant is looking for in a sales job and his or her salary requirements. If you like the candidate's telephone personality, try to obtain at least three references.

- *Reference check.*   Call each reference and try to get secondary references (references from these references who also know the candidate—a former subordinate, peer, or boss). This is the *key reference* whom the applicant usually will not give you.

If you are talented and lucky, you should be able to eliminate about 75 percent of the applicants at this stage of the selection process. Now you can focus your attention on the remaining high-potential candidates.

The Rep Who Was Too Independent

Sometimes a flake filters through even the most sophisticated screening systems. Mark Twain said it best: "Barring that natural expression of villainy which we all have, the man looked honest enough." This maverick from Missoula managed to hire himself out as a full-time salesperson (11 western states) to four different Eastern manufacturers. He used assumed names and different social security numbers and mailing addresses with each firm. As part of each company's compensation package, he received a brand-new automobile and a plush expense account.

In addition to normal travel expenses and customer entertainment, he usually wined and dined his friends and relatives on a regular basis. Each big night out on the town was duly written up as a "legitimate" business expense and submitted to all four principal firms on a regular rotating basis. To make matters worse, he rented out three of his four company cars. He was living pretty high on the hog.

Because of poor screening and selection procedures and infrequent field follow-up and supervision by the sales managers of each of his four employers, this unscrupulous manipulator got away with this scam for years. He would probably still be doing it if one of his rented automobiles hadn't gotten stolen. Then his whole dishonest scheme "hit the fan," and he wound up in jail, where he belonged. Here was a rep who was just a little bit too independent for his own good.

When Is the Best Time to Recruit Mavericks?

Any time is the best time. As previously stated, recruiting should be a continuous process because of normal and anticipated attrition in any sales organization. If there is a best time, it would be when everything is going great guns, when your sales volume and staff morale are at their highest. Don't make the fatal mistake of waiting until you have a problem in one of your territories, sales volume is low, or a maverick terminates, defects, or rides off into the sunset. It is certainly a lot easier to convince applicants to sell for you if they see and feel sagebrush success all around them. Nobody, no matter how desperate, wants to work for a company that seems like a loser. Therefore, *any* time can be your best time to recruit mavericks. Just get into the habit of doing it. Having frequent cattle calls will stock your corral to capacity with these prime products.

Chapter 5 Roundup

How can you be assured that you will recruit the maverick sales superstars whom you seek rather than Darwin's ape? Appropriate human resource planning for all of your territories is the answer. This chapter was chock-full of information about this cattle-calling process and contained ideas on how to screen out prairie dogs and other organizational misfits. Objectives of effective recruiting and selection were covered along with the importance of staff retention and the prohibitive cost of employee turnover.

After assessing your individual sales territory shortcomings and requirements, you must determine rep qualifications, define successful job performance, and establish job specifications. Some terrain is trickier than others and their inhabitants more hostile and widespread. All of these variables must be factored into your final job description. When you finish writing it all down, ask yourself if you would take the job. If your honest answer is yes, then you are now ready to move on to the interviewing table. If your response is no, then it's back to the drawing boards.

How you approach this planning stage depends upon your own psychological personality profile. But, whatever your style, recruiting should be an ongoing process in order to ensure stable organizational growth and development. Put Darwin's theory of natural selection to work for you. These are the preinterviewing activities that will pay off.

6
Conducting Effective Interviews

One man that has a mind and knows it can
always beat ten men who haven't and don't.
GEORGE BERNARD SHAW

Introduction to Interviewing

How are you going to find that one man or woman who has a mind and knows it and screen out the ten mindless wonders who will darken your doorway? This is the challenge of maverick interviewing—one of your most important doing activities. (As discussed in Chap. 2, it's okay to "do," as long as you know that you are *doing* rather than *managing* and that you don't overdo it! There is always the temptation to climb back into the saddle and start doing everything all by yourself, so you've always got to establish priorities and clearly differentiate between the two.)

Now that the planning and organizing steps in the recruiting process have been completed, you must don your buyer's cap and your most diagnostic frame of mind. You are about to make the second biggest purchase of your life (after your ranch): you are going to buy the services of a professional salesperson.

Why Are Some Sales Managers Such Ineffective Interviewers?

Sales managers who don't conduct interviews well may be inexperienced or lack training in this crucial area; their personalities and value systems are also important factors. Depending upon your psychological personality profile, as an interviewer, you are going to make various kinds of mistakes and outright blunders. If you are an affiliator/pleaser by nature, you will adore just about anybody who stumbles into your office and try to build a friendly relationship with them. You belong to the Will Rogers school of people pleasers. Did you ever meet a man or woman you didn't like? If an applicant is late or doesn't have a résumé, you will most likely make excuses for them, saying that it really didn't matter and not to worry. You will do most of the talking and frequently get off the track. Your interviews will run past their allotted appointment times, and you are never on schedule or keep to your agenda. You probably view the placement interview as another social function in which you are the goodwill ambassador of your company. Many times it's so difficult to choose from among so many beautiful people, and you feel badly about having to reject anyone. You feel certain, however, that one day they, too, will qualify for membership in your wonderful sales team.

If you are a power boss/commander, you respond to strong personalities like yourself and are often more impressed by a firm handshake than by solid credentials. You never waste time with wimps or losers, tend to do all of the talking—usually about yourself and your heroic sales exploits—and are prone to make snap judgments based on gut feel and intuition. Your overall batting average is pretty good, so you don't mess around with a lot of stupid home office forms and paperwork. You're pretty fast on the draw. You can spot a winner when you see one.

An avoider/abdicator sales manager approaches the interviewing process in a much more cautious and clinical manner. Here, you will be most interested in "getting the facts and finding the gaps" in an applicant's job history so that you can find an excuse for rejecting him or her. Meeting strangers is a painful experience for you and must be deferred for as long as possible. You would love to abdicate this odious activity completely and let someone else do it for you. Once compelled to this "dirty work," you know that you will never shake hands with your applicants or look them in the eyes. You believe in the Navigator Theory of Recruitment which holds that you cannot tell where a candidate is going in his or her career unless you know where he or she has been. "Winners tend to become winners, while losers continue to lose, so why is he or she looking for a job?"

You hate change and wonder why so many of these mavericks job-hop. You're afraid of making a hiring boner, so you demand reams of information from each candidate, starting with their earliest childhood experiences. This will enable you to cover your ass if you accidentally hire a loser or justify your failure to hire *anyone* for the job. If you *do* hire someone, they certainly won't be power boss/commanders or affiliator/pleasers—bad for company image!

Achiever/technicians are equally interested in getting the facts, but they will use that information—rather than hide behind it—to find the best-qualified mavericks on the range. If this is your personality style, you will emphasize a candidate's educational background, technical training, and work experience over their human skills. You will ask a lot of pertinent questions, take prolific notes, and keep strictly to your agenda and interviewing schedule. If an applicant asks the right questions and uses the right buzz words, you know that you are going to love 'em.

A manipulator/facilitator views the interviewing process as an integral part of his or her long-term career game plan. Here is an opportunity for you to size up these prospective range riders in terms of their possible use to you now as well as in the future. Will they be friends, foes, allies, competitors, or protégés? Which of these mavericks will ascend to positions of power and influence in your company or industry?

You will ask them a few loaded questions to test their technical and conceptual thinking without seeming to note their responses. You'll set them at ease by adapting your personality to match theirs and be very courteous and low-keyed—except to a power boss/commander applicant. You will allow these hopefuls to do most of the talking, but you will indirectly control the interview through a series of adroit questions and astute comments. Your final selection decision—like everything else you do—will be pragmatic.

Interviewing Ineffectiveness
Summary

Most sales managers are influenced by bias and stereotyping of job applicants based on their own personalities. They tend to project their needs on others and usually wind up hiring mavericks who are like themselves. This compounds their organizational strengths and weaknesses and is the basis for many corporate cultures, often extending to the choice of dress and hobbies. Listen to a PB/C on the subject: "Only a wimp would go to a ballet, we're going hunting. We shoot coyotes with Uzis!"

Some sales managers are uncertain about the kinds of information that they should give or receive in interviews. When they finally get the desired data, these executives misinterpret it, sometimes playing amateur psychiatrist with either disastrous or hilarious results. Others allow the candidate to control the interview, tend to talk too much, or telegraph the desired responses to their questions. It all boils down to a lack of preparation and a lack of an organized approach to interviewing.

How Many Interviews and How Much Time?

For each finalist who survives your preinterview screening process, I recommend two or three interviews, 30 to 60 minutes for the first session, 1½ to 2 hours for the second, and possibly a half to a full day for the last, if necessary. Suggested topical areas and allotted times are as follows:

	Time allocation, min	
Topic	First session	Second session
Work history and selling experience	30	50
Education and technical training	10	15
Early home background	10	15
Present social adjustment	5	10
Self-evaluation	5	15
Total	60	105

Naturally, you will use your own good judgment regarding the length of your interview as well as the timing of its various segments. Achiever/technician sales managers will stick closely to this format and finish each interview exactly on schedule. Power boss/commanders knock off early, avoider/abdicators take their own sweet time, affiliator/pleasers run over, and manipulator/facilitators vary the speed and intensity based on the interviewee's needs and their own objectives.

Depending upon the nature of the position and the personality of the applicant, a third interview might be scheduled at the home office, where several other executives would be involved in the game.

Who Should Do the Interviewing?

Good question. The first meeting or screening interview could be done by yourself, one of your trusted ranch hands (regional managers), mavericks (senior salespeople), or a qualified human resources department executive. Once the minimum employment requirements have been established, it is not difficult for any of these experienced executives to screen out the stumblebums.

Rather than find this chore a burden, the staff members whom you involve in interviewing may be motivated by your interest in them — particularly your achiever/technician and manipulator/facilitator mavericks. Therefore, delegate this initial interviewing activity without compunctions.

Communicate Your Objectives Up Front

The employment interview is the initial phase of what will hopefully become a long-term business relationship between you and your new mavericks. You have ascertained beforehand what you expect from your new salespeople, and you must now communicate those objectives and requirements during the very first interview. Put all of your recruiting cards out on the table. If you hire new reps without telling them exactly what you expect from them in terms of job performance, how can you ever have a meaningful job appraisal session later on? In other words, without clear-cut objectives — explicitly communicated to your applicants up front — how will either of you ever know whether or not the applicant, as a new employee, has reached a satisfactory performance level? Furthermore, any effective monitoring of progress toward a poorly defined or nonexistent goal is virtually impossible.

Upon learning of your job requirements, some prospects will disqualify themselves from further consideration.

"You mean I have to travel?"

"It's a *straight commission* job?"

"I've got to pay my own expenses?"

Communicate your job objectives up front and level with your candidates. It will save you both a lot of time.

Interviewing Guidelines: Asking the Right Questions

Before you sit down at the interviewing table to negotiate any job, you should be armed with a series of questions that will unmask impostors and single out promising candidates. These penetrating questions can be developed from a survey of the best mavericks in your own company or industry. If your trade association or professional organization does not provide this service, you can either buy it from an outside research firm or have your own human resources department conduct the survey.

If you know what your best mavericks like best about their positions and what they consider are their best personal attributes, you can develop a series of questions that will rope in candidates who have similar attitudes, abilities, and attributes while cutting out those stragglers who don't. To be even more certain, you can take this method one step further by surveying the sales managers in your industry regarding their top salespeople's best personal assets and behavioral patterns. You can even query purchasing agents and other customer-contact people for their criteria.

How to Use This Technique

A recent study of the best sales reps in the electronics industry indicated what these superior mavericks like most about their jobs. Ranked in order of their stated preferences were:

1. *Working with people.*   Helping customers
2. *Accomplishment.*   Closing orders, prestige, recognition
3. *Challenge.*   Winning the "numbers game" and breaking new ground
4. *Variety.*   Creating own progress, being own boss, working with peers, and independence

They said that their best personal assets — ranked by order of stated preference — were:

1. *Knowledge of people.*   Empathy and perception, selling ability, thoughtfulness, and good listening skills
2. *Follow through.*   Persistence and good organization
3. *Personality.*   Appearance, enthusiasm, flexibility, positive attitude, luck, self-control, and good memory

4. *Drive.* Ambition, competition, hard work, curiosity, aggression, and pride

5. *Integrity.*

6. *Engineering background.* Product knowledge

7. *Intelligence.* Innovation

What these reps' sales managers said were their top salespeople's prime personal assets differed somewhat in the ranked order of importance.

1. *Personality.* Enthusiasm and liking for people

2. *Integrity.*

3. *Planning.* Persistence, customer service, follow through, and initiative

4. *Hard work.* Pleasure in work, self-sacrifice, and high energy level

5. *Aggressiveness.* Ego involvement

6. *Product knowledge.*

7. *Selling ability.* Good closer and communication skills

8. *Intelligence.*

How would you rank order the best personal assets of your most successful mavericks? Figure 6-1 summarizes the most important attributes of successful salespeople in the electronics industry survey and the questions which were developed from the data. Interviewers could then ask smart questions that would enable them to ascertain whether their sales applicants possessed those most desired and identifiable success qualities. You can use this format as a guideline for developing your own company or industry-related interviewing questions.

How to Read between the Lines of a Résumé

Next to your mavericks' expense account reports, an applicant's résumé is probably the most creative work of fiction you're ever going to have to read in the West. Some are put together with transparent mending tape and coffee stains, while others are the work of professional résumé services and employment agencies. Therefore, you want to be able to penetrate this professional facade to distinguish between truth and fantasy and whether you are dealing with the genuine rawhide article. Here are

Figure 6-1. Questions to ask prospective salespeople to determine if they possess the most important attributes of a successful salesperson.

Questions to Ask Prospective Salespeople

Factors which the best salespeople said that they liked most about selling	Questions to ask applicants	What to look for in answers
Working with people	What were your favorite courses in school? Why?	Courses that involve relationships and creativity, rather than science, accounting, etc.
	What was your favorite job? Why?	Those working with people
	What are your hobbies? Why?	Social hobbies, such as team sports, bridge or recreations, rather than solitary hobbies, such as stamp or butterfly collecting and others which are more private in nature.
Accomplishment	What do you feel is your most outstanding accomplishment? Why?	Does this involve people? Does it involve selling? What kind of feeling do they show when they tell you about this accomplishment? How *big* is it?
Meeting the challenge	What is the biggest challenge you've ever had?	Look for enthusiasm when they tell you about it. How difficult was it? How well did they prepare themselves? What was the result? Did they plan?
Variety on the job	What kind of a business day would please you most?	Determine whether they like routine, nonroutine, or challenging activities.
	Would you rather be a cowpuncher or a ranch hand? Why?	Note any desire for creativity, being their own boss, and avoiding routine. Are they too proud to cut hay but not wild enough to eat it?

Making money	If you had your choice, would you rather work on straight commission or straight salary?	Look for salespeople who want to work on commission. (If you only offer straight salary, don't ask this question.) Are they recognition-oriented or security-motivated?
Ability to handle people	No question is really needed here. Study the effect your applicants are having on you. After all, this is one of the most important sales that they can make.	Have they been listening to you? How do they react when you speak? Are they "turning you on" or "off"? Would you buy a used car from this maverick?
Ability to follow through	What are the most important things that you feel a customer looks for in a salesperson?	They should be describing service, follow-through, and genuine interest in the customer by the salesperson. If they don't, something might be missing.
Personality and drive	How would you describe your own personality?	Do they mention handling people, empathy, follow-through, enthusiasm, positive mental attitude, drive, and ambition? Which of the five personality types is this applicant?
Integrity	Given a free hand, how far do you think a salesperson should go in entertainment and gifts to buyers?	How do their responses fit with your company policies?
	How do you feel about the pay-offs you've been reading about from the big corporations to the governments and the recent congressional scandals?	Are they indignant, passive, or evasive? Will they wind up hustling business or rustling cattle? You don't want any fence straddlers in your outfit.

some probing inquiries which you can use that a headhunter could not have prepared them for in advance.

1. How many sales calls are you accustomed to making in one day?
2. What do you feel is your real potential?
3. What do you know about our firm?
4. Why do you want to work for us?
5. What makes you think that you would be successful with *our* product line?
6. What book or article have you read on selling lately?
7. How would you define selling?
8. Which selling techniques seem to work best for you?

You might also ask the applicant to "sell" something to you. This mock sale will enable you to evaluate the speed with which the applicant thinks, his or her creativity, and perhaps even behavioral tendencies. A variation of this scenario is as follows: "Suppose you have to leave this office right away to sell a new and totally unfamiliar product door-to-door. If you can only ask three things about this product before you go, what would they be?"

There is, of course, no right or wrong answer, just your own impressions of the applicant's impromptu responses. Thus, when probing your applicant's résumé, it's important to listen to *how* this individual replies as well as *what* he or she says. Careful observation allows you to assess the candidate's potential strengths and perhaps his or her untapped potential.

If the prospect is able to survive this probing scrutiny, then you have a promising candidate with whom you will want to proceed further. It is now time to "sell" him or her on the job opportunity, so put on your best pair of cowboy boots, strap on your gun belt, and take careful aim at your target.

Your Ethics Are on the Line

If integrity and ethics are high on your list for appraising range riders' job performances, then be careful that you take the same medicine yourself and don't exaggerate potential earnings or future promotional opportunities. How many times have they heard about El Dorado and the never-never land of opportunity? If it's a dead-end job, tell 'em. Don't dangle the bait about nonexistent management openings or try to pull the wool over their eyes.

Don't brag about the kind of car you drive, the size of your house, or your high standard of living. Applicants aren't interested in your success, only what they can earn and accomplish on the job. Therefore, you must always give as accurate and honest a picture of your sales position as possible. Remember, your ethics are on the line and the "book" on you travels around your industry pretty fast.

Legal Considerations: Uncle Sam Is Listening

Interviewing shares some features with the game of Monopoly. Ask the wrong questions; go directly to jail. Do not pass GO. Do not collect $200. Most likely the sheriff will be after you and your firm with fines exceeding many thousands of dollars. In other words, some inquiries are illegal. Therefore, it is your responsibility to know which questions can be asked without violating your applicants' rights under the various laws against discrimination in employment. Since the burden of proof is always on the interviewing company—and you are their agent—you had better lend an ear to your firm's legal and human resources departments and stop asking nosy questions. These staff members can provide valuable assistance in complying with governmental requirements. In addition, Fig. 6-2 lists some of the most important employment-related laws with which you should be familiar. Remember, an employer is *responsible* for discrimination on the part of individual supervisors like sales managers and other company recruiters. The Equal Employment Opportunity Commission (EEOC) will consider questions on the following subjects as evidence of discrimination unless you are able to explain satisfactorily that they are *not* used for that purpose. In addition, Fig. 6-3 gives you the full array of interviewing "commandments."

1. *Arrest and conviction records.* These are viewed as discriminatory because blacks and other minorities have a higher percentage of arrests than nonminorities.

2. *Garnishment records.* Questions on this subject are considered discriminatory for the same reason.

3. *Credit references.*

4. *Marital status.* You may not ask about marital status unless you ask the same question of both men and women. It is permissible to ask whether "Mr." "Mrs." or "Miss," if it is for a nondiscriminatory purpose.

5. *Child care problems.* Again, you may only ask about child care arrangements if the question is asked of both men and women.

6. *Contraceptive practices.* Questions such as "What kind of birth control methods do you use?" and the like are illegal.

7. *Plans to have children.*

Laws Which You Should Know

1. *Title VII of the Civil Rights Act of 1964.* This law applies to employers with 15 or more employees and bans all discrimination on the basis of race, color, religion, sex, or national origin. It covers all terms and conditions of employment and holds employers responsible for any discrimination that goes on within their organizations. Title VII is administered and enforced by the Equal Employment Opportunity Commission.

2. *Equal Pay Act of 1963.* The Equal Pay Act forbids pay differentials on the basis of sex. It is enforced by the Wage and Hour division of the Department of Labor.

3. *Age Discrimination in Employment Act.* This act bans discrimination because of age against anyone at least 40 years old but less than 65. It is enforced by the Equal Employment Opportunity Commission since 1979.

4. *Executive Order 11246.* This order covers all employers with government contracts or subcontracts of more than $10,000. It requires that every contract contain a clause against discrimination because of race, color, sex, religion, or national origin. In addition, Revised Order Number 4, based on Executive Order 11246, requires contractors and subcontractors with 50 or more employees and a contract of $50,000 or more to develop and carry out a written affirmative action program. This executive order is enforced by 18 federal contracting agencies that have been designated compliance agencies by the Labor Department's Office of Federal Contract Compliance.

Figure 6-2. The sales manager should be familiar with the most important employment-related laws.

8. *Unwed motherhood.*

9. *Age.* This is a forbidden subject because this information can be used to violate the Age Discrimination in Employment Act.

10. *Type of military discharge.*

11. *Height and weight.*

12. *Other potential areas of discrimination.* These include education, physical requirements, availability for weekend work, friends or relatives working for the same company, and appearance.

Thou shalt not

1. Ask the applicants if he or she has worked under another name.
2. Ask for his or her birthplace or those of close relatives.
3. Ask the applicant's age.
4. Reference his or her church or social or fraternal affiliations.
5. Ask if the applicant has ever been arrested.
6. Ask that a photo be submitted with a résumé.
7. Ask if the applicant will cross a picket line.
8. Violate the applicant's right under the Fair Credit Reporting Act.
9. Indicate any discrimination based on race, color, religion, sex, age, or national origin in your company advertising.
10. Refuse to hire because an applicant has filed charges or testified in any actions under Title VII.
11. Refuse to hire because of race, color, religion, sex, age, or national origin.

Thou shalt

1. Advertise for a position (not a man).
2. Select a skill (not an age group).
3. Hire a salesperson (not a color or sex).

Figure 6-3. These do's and don'ts will help the sales manager avoid asking any questions that might be perceived as discriminatory.

How Can You Protect Yourself?

Delegate. Get your human resources and legal departments into the act. Have them help you to prepare a list of questions that you can ask applicants about their qualifications, experience, and background without violating their rights under the various laws against discrimination in employment. In ascertaining whether the questions you are preparing to ask your interviewees are legal, the EEOC suggests that you first ask yourself the following questions:

1. Does this question tend to have a disproportionate effect in screening out minorities and women?
2. Is this information really necessary to judge this person's competence for the performance of this particular job?
3. Are there alternative, nondiscriminatory ways to secure the necessary information?

Remember, only those questions which establish the applicant's qualifications for the job are approved by the federal government. When the government challenges a hiring practice, the burden of proof lies squarely on the shoulders of the accused company. Now that you are an expert on the subject, test your memory and judgment with the Lawful Interview Self-Quiz which concludes this chapter. The correct answers are to be found in your Sales Manager's Manual (Chap. 13).

Interviewing Sequences

Before an applicant can seriously be considered for employment, he or she must successfully progress through at least two different kinds of interviews: the screening interview and the selection interview. They differ in terms of length, content, objectives, and intensity. Under special circumstances, a third and final interview might be scheduled.

The Screening Interview

The purpose of this session is to screen out those applicants who are obviously unqualified for your available selling position and to screen in those who are, so that mutually convenient appointment times for the selection interview can be arranged. If you have delegated the résumé-screening job to a subordinate and you wind up seeing too many unqualified people, you know that you have a staff training problem or that your instructions were not clear.

Schedule appointments far enough apart so that neither you nor the applicant will feel rushed, and allow enough time to make notes before or after each interview. Ensure privacy in your office or conference room without allowing any interruptions. Create a warm and friendly atmosphere so that you can establish rapport. Listen to and observe your visitor, take notes, combine data, and then conclude the meeting. That's the general outline; here are some specifics.

Introduction

Be prompt and courteous. After a cordial greeting and some small talk to relax the applicant, you could begin with this opening statement:

> Thank you for coming. We're here together today to discuss the position that's open, and to see whether it is the right one for you. This should be a discovery process for us both. I'm going to ask you some questions now, and you will have an opportunity to ask me some later.

You then proceed to ask the applicant a series of questions which are designed to draw him or her out so that you can get to the person as an individual. You will utilize comprehensive introductory, follow-up, and open-ended questions. Avoid yes or no questions.

Comprehensive introductory questions are almost all-inclusive: they should spell out most of the main factors which you need to know about your candidate's selling and other pertinent experience. *Follow-up questions* are an extension of the comprehensive question: they encourage elaboration. *Open-ended questions* cannot be answered with a yes or a no.

Listen carefully to the candidate's responses, give encouragement, play down unfavorable information, and inject a little humor along the way. It is important that you treat all of your interviewees—whether qualified or not—in a friendly and courteous manner. You should be listening and observing 85 percent of the time, while speaking only 15 percent of the interview time. This makes sense to avoider/abdicator, achiever/technician, and manipulator/facilitator sales managers, but is considered to be "utter rubbish" by power boss/commanders and affiliator/pleasers. How do you feel about it?

Concluding the Screening Interview

If you've got a "live one," you'll want to move quickly. "Close" for the second, or selection, interview. If there's mutual interest, arrange the second meeting as soon as possible, especially for applicants who have come from out of town. Candidates whom you have rejected at this stage should be thanked for their time and interest and promptly notified of your decision. *Never leave an applicant dangling in suspense.* It is not fair to them and reflects unfavorably on you and your company. Always be professional and do the right thing in the right way. That's part of the Interviewing Code of the Old West.

The Selection Interview

The second interview is a selection session and should be longer and more intensive than the screening interview. You've got some promising prospects who look like they can handle the job, but you want to be absolutely sure. Through the course of this meeting, you ask another barrage of smart questions which are designed to draw out more relevant facts and information. Their responses will enable you to better assess their qualifications against your previously established job-related behavioral success criteria. Here are some examples.

1. How do you spend your spare time? (You want to know the applicant's interests, get a feel for behavioral patterns and the balance in his or her life.)

2. How does this sales job compare with others for which you have applied?

3. What makes the difference between success and failure?

4. What would you say are your best qualities?

5. What do people usually criticize you for?

6. For what do you criticize them?

7. What did you especially like about your last sales job?

8. What was your favorite sales manager like?

9. What was your least favorite boss like?

10. How did previous employers treat you?

11. What have you done that shows initiative and willingness to work?

12. Describe your biggest sale. (Note how much of it was through his or her own efforts.)

13. What is the most difficult thing you have ever done? (Note how "difficult" it was, and how much stress was involved.)

14. What is the most gratifying thing you have ever done?

15. If you could have chosen any career, what would it have been? Why?

16. Why did you choose your particular line of work? Why selling for a career?

17. What would you say constitutes a good sales approach?

18. How would you make a given day in selling be the most effective? (Is the word *planning* mentioned?)

19. What has stopped you from getting ahead more quickly?

20. What are some of the aspects of selling that you dislike?

21. Did you have much paperwork in your last sales job? (Note how he or she handled it.)

22. When you took your last sales position, where did you see yourself in five years? (Is "goal-setting" mentioned?)

23. What does it take to be a top salesperson?

24. What does *success* mean to you?

25. How do you like to be managed?

26. If you were to become a sales manager one day, what would be your style of management?

27. How would you rate yourself on a scale of 1 to 10? Why?

28. Why did you decide to change jobs?

29. What do you hope to gain from a sales organization like ours?

30. When you analyze yourself in relation to your track record and those of other salespeople, do you find some areas that need improvement? If so, what are they, and how would you go about doing it?

The Turning Point

If these tough questions are answered to your satisfaction, you might have a winner. Immediately proceed to the next step, which is giving detailed job, territory, and company information. Provide this contender with a factual basis for accepting or rejecting the job, if it is offered to him or her. Now you don your salesperson cap and start selling this qualified candidate on all the reasons why he or she should become a new member of your sales team. Observe his or her reactions and try to get a commitment. Make sure that he or she *wants* the job. If so, and if your *positive* feelings are reinforced by the additional information that you have extracted from this second session, you will make a decision. Your choices are to hire the applicant on the spot, reject him or her, or schedule additional interviewing.

If a third and final interview is scheduled—usually at the home office—at least four executives should be involved in the process. Your prime candidate or candidates will spend about an hour with your

Director of human resources

Vice president of marketing

One of your field assistants, regional managers, or sales managers-in-training

Yourself

The candidate must sell himself or herself to all of these different functional people. Afterwards, you and your fellow executives will compare notes and impressions. You, of course, will make the final hiring decision.

Concluding the Interview
on an Upbeat Note

Once the desired information exchange has been completed and your interviewing objectives have been reached, you should terminate the interview in a pleasant and courteous manner. Your closing comments could be as follows: "Thank you for visiting with me today. I've enjoyed talking with you and getting to know you. As you know, I'm interviewing others for the position, so I will be getting back to you within two weeks."

The ball is in your court. Do not ask them to call you back to see if they got the job. This is most unprofessional, and most applicants will be reluctant to risk rejection over the telephone. You want them all to leave your office feeling good about you, your company, and their interviewing experience. Who knows when you might meet again and under what circumstances? Jimmy Durante once quipped, "Be nice to people on your way up, because you'll meet 'em on your way down."

Chapter 6 Roundup

The personal interview is the most important selection tool available to sales managers. Nothing beats a face-to-face meeting. A structured approach to interviewing enables you to evaluate candidate qualifications against proven success criteria for your sales positions. Using smart questions and listening and observation skills will help you to size up the winners and screen out the losers.

Depending upon the size and nature of your firm, the degree of urgency to fill an open territory, and the number of applicants from which to choose, you will probably schedule two or three personal interviews before you make a job offer. All of your interviewing activities should be conducted in a professional and legal manner. That's part of the Code of the Old West.

Lawful Interview Self-Quiz

This little quiz will test your knowledge regarding the important factors involved in designing and asking questions for a lawful employment interview.

1. Under Title VII of the Civil Rights Act, the employer is not responsible for discrimination on the part of individual supervisors, like sales managers.

True _____ False _____

2. The Equal Pay Act forbids pay differentials on the basis of sex.

True _____ False _____

3. The Age Discrimination in Employment Act does not protect employees who are between 35 and 40 years old.

True _____ False _____

4. Some state fair employment practice laws ban practices that are not expressly forbidden by federal laws.

True _____ False _____

5. When charged with discrimination, employers must prove that their standards and requirements are reasonably necessary for job performance.

True _____ False _____

6. Any standards or qualifications that the employer wants to establish will be accepted as bona fide occupational qualifications by the Equal Employment Opportunity Commission.

True _____ False _____

7. The validation procedure prescribed by the Equal Employment Opportunity Commission applies to preemployment tests alone.

True _____ False _____

8. It is never permissible for an employer to set height and weight requirements for a job.

True _____ False _____

9. An employer must make allowances for an employee's religious practices unless undue hardship would result.

True _____ False _____

(Continued)

10. It is never considered discriminatory to ask about an applicant's work experience.

True _____ False _____

11. A rule that only one partner in a marriage may work for the same company might be considered discriminatory.

True_____ False_____

12. Employers are within their rights if they routinely screen out male job applicants with long hair.

True_____ False_____

13. Questions about an applicant's military experience or training are permitted.

True_____ False_____

14. It is always permissible to refuse to hire an alien.

True_____ False_____

15. It is unwise to tell unsuccessful candidates the reason why they were not hired.

True_____ False_____

7
Postinterviewing Activities

Many are called, but few are chosen.
MATTHEW 22:14

Introduction: High Noon at the Hiring Corral

It's getting close to decision time, and the hiring clock is ticking. The sales territory is still open, and you've narrowed it down to a few serious contenders. Before you put your brand on your new maverick, there are other selection tools at your disposal. They will either validate or contradict the information that you have derived from each of these prime prospects during the interviewing process. Postinterviewing activities can save you from making some very costly hiring mistakes. Prepare yourself, it's high noon at the hiring corral.

Interpretation of Information and Impressions

Review your notes, compare your impressions with others who have also interviewed these front-runners on your "short list." *Can* they do the job? How do their individual qualifications and selling experiences mesh with your present job requirements? *Will* they do the job? What kind of impression did their personalities make on you? Did they "turn you on," or "off"? Will they have a positive impact on your customers? Will they fit in with your other mavericks? In other words, is he or she your kind of salesperson, the best-qualified candidate for the job? You don't want to wind up hiring a bunch of Montgomery Ward mail-order mavericks.

Even if you are absolutely sold on one specific individual, you've still got to check out the references, consider testing the candidate, and maybe meet his or her spouse. These other selection tools will give you a more balanced approach to hiring and also serve as a check on your own personal bias and prejudices. Never limit yourself to fewer than three finalists because some may become disqualified at the eleventh hour and others may reject your offer.

The Fine Art of Reference Checking

If the personal interview is the most important selection tool, then reference checking is a close second. References can verify statements made on the application form or in person and provide additional data which could influence your final hiring decision. You should obtain three to five references that can be drawn from the following:

1. A key former customer
2. A subordinate who worked for the applicant
3. A superior, their previous sales manager
4. A fellow salesperson or other employee
5. The key reference whom the candidate will usually *not* give you (another person from someone in the first four categories who also knows your prospect)

Applicants usually provide the names of people who will give them high marks, but as mentioned in Chap. 5, your task is to probe for a third party whom the reference knows and who has sufficient working knowledge of your candidate to give an informed opinion. This is your key reference. Get him or her, and you deserve the Golden Spur Award.

The best time to check out these references is immediately after the selection interview concludes and you have obtained permission from your applicant. A personal visit to his or her former employer's office or a telephone call are preferred to writing letters. Because of legal considerations, references are reluctant to put anything in writing for fear of lawsuits. In person, you will be better able to obtain detailed information about the candidate regarding dates of employment, earnings, attendance record, nature of the applicant's duties, how he or she got along with fellow sales team members and customers, and reasons for leaving the job. You can also observe the reference's nonverbal reactions to your queries.

When speaking with a candidate's former employers, the key question to ask is: "Would you rehire her or him?" Neutral responses are considered negative. All information received through reference checking is strictly confidential and should never be divulged to applicants or other people. Complete confidentiality in these delicate matters is part of the Code of the Old West.

Power boss and avoider sales managers aren't too keen on references as reliable sources of validation information. "Range riders are a dime a dozen, and all they ever give you are friends, relatives, or old drinking buddies. Would they ever give you a bad reference? Somebody who would say what a bum they really are?" These executives much prefer checking with their own industry connections — their sales management network, credit reports, special investigating firms, and applicant driving records.

Affiliator sales managers love to gossip with references, while achievers and manipulators put this personal interviewing time to maximum usage. The ever time-conscious achiever would prefer to handle reference checks over the telephone so that other work could also be done simultaneously.

To Test or Not to Test?

Although power boss and affiliator sales managers feel that all tests are "for the birds," achievers, avoiders, and manipulators think that they can be a very valuable selection tool. Tests can objectively identify and quantify significant mental ability and personality traits that are not normally measured by the application blank, background check, and personal interview.

Depending upon the nature of your sales position, its requirements and company policy, you can choose from among the following kinds of examinations:

1. Intelligence or mental ability tests

2. Interest tests

3. Mechanical aptitude tests

4. Sales aptitude tests

5. Personality tests

All that these tests can tell you—within certain limitations—is what applicants *can do* but not necessarily what they *will do* under actual field selling conditions. As you well know, there is a world of difference between knowing what to do in a given selling situation and actually being able to do it. How many times have you interviewed a "hot shot" who looked like a winner, talked like a winner, but performed like a loser? This is the Howard LaFlash—the flash-in-the-pan from our case study in Chap. 4. These con artists are merely good at interviewing, nothing else.

Remember, a test is no better than the people who design, administer, and interpret the data. These esoteric activities should be handled by company experts such as your human resources department specialists and staff psychologists or outside professional resources. The key considerations in testing are twofold:

- *Is this test valid?*   Does it measure what it purports to measure? Does it measure what you want it to measure?

- *Is this test reliable?*   If a maverick were to take this test more than once, would he or she score within the same range each time? How consistent are the results over an extended period of time?

Testing, if properly developed, administered, and interpreted, can play a vital role in the selection process because it eliminates interviewer bias and personality stereotyping.

The Dangers of Testing

One of the most devastating arguments against testing is that it may eliminate truly creative sales candidates and individuals with sales management potential. Most mavericks do poorly on tests but sell superbly in the field. Some people are great at taking tests but nothing else. Just as there are professional interviewers, there are professional test takers. It's their true vocation!

In addition, many of the complaints filed under Title VII of the Civil Rights Act charge that tests have been used in ways that result in unfair discrimination against members of minority groups and women.

Avoider/abdicator sales managers make the all-too-frequent mistake of thinking that psychological tests are the *actual* selector of salespeople. Tests are "safe" to hide behind, because they cannot be challenged. After all, the test results speak for themselves, and who are they—or anyone else—to argue with the experts? It's an easy way out.

In the final analysis, *tests should only be used as an aid to judgment* and not as the primary deciding factor in determining who should be hired and who should be rejected. The personal interview and prior selling experience of the applicant should take precedence over any test results.

Should You Interview an Applicant's Spouse?

Affiliator/pleaser sales managers simply adore this idea because it is a chance to make a new friend. It's another fun social occasion on the good old company expense account. Other sales manager personality types have varying opinions of its value. The main objective of the spouse interview is to ascertain whether an applicant's home life has a positive or a negative influence upon him or her. Another goal of this informal session is to make certain that the spouse clearly understands those aspects of the job that might have a significant impact on the candidate's family lifestyle. Selling on the range is rough enough by itself. Without a spouse's wholehearted support, many a maverick has failed to make the grade.

Dinner out together (neutral ground) or at the prospect's home (their turf) are the best places to meet. The chuck wagon at their homestead is the preferred location because you can appraise their standard of living and also place the spouse in familiar surroundings. Hopefully he or she will tend to relax and speak more freely. Among the things that you will want to learn are:

How does the spouse envision his or her role in the family?

Who wears the bronc belt or cracks the whip at home?

Is he or she supportive, competitive, dominant, passive, etc.?

What are the attitudes of the spouse and the rest of the family toward the job?

Toward the company?

How do they feel about its products and policies?

Are there any aspects of the sales position which they find undesirable?

What are their attitudes toward selling, in general?

Do they consider it a desirable career?

What job-related goals has the spouse set for the applicant, or vice versa?

Do they desire more than the job and your company can reasonably offer?

As the author O. Henry observed about job-hunters in a tight labor market: "You're the goods." Be assured that both the candidate and spouse know his or her current market value; they've been coached by professionals. That is another reason why you must clarify *all* aspects of the position before you conclude this informal meeting and tender a job offer.

Knock-Out Factors

Extreme job-hopping, a poor track record, willingness to accept a sharp reduction in earnings from a previous job, negative spouse, or too many qualifications are red flags that should preclude any further consideration. How many Ph.D.s in advanced technology really *want* to get down into the mud puddle, put on the crash helmet, and sell *anything* for a living?

Applicants with a recent business failure or a family business in their background are usually looking for a temporary refuge until they can either get back on their feet financially or become reconciled with their family business. They are "buying time," and you are paying the bill. Poor physical appearance, chronic health, and alcohol or drug abuse problems are other knock-out factors. (*A word of caution: Appearance* has been used over the years as a code word for racial or religious backgrounds that were undesirable to companies and was routinely used to deny applicants fair access to jobs. Don't fall into that trap.)

Physical Exams and Drug Testing

This is a tough one. Company policy might require all job candidates to submit to physical exams and drug tests before they can be hired. Play it safe. Ask *all* of your sales applicants to take these tests, but be absolutely certain that these company requirements will not violate federal or state statutes.

Drug testing and alcohol abuse are murky areas. Both issues are much more subtle than physical fitness considerations because they do not usually emerge until *after* employment commences. Sometimes you can spot an "alki" during a lunch or dinner interview by the number, speed, and volume of drinks that he or she consumes in a social setting. A ruddy complexion and facial veining can also be telltale signs but are not always reliable. Most alcoholics are clever enough to cover their tracks and control themselves during the interviewing process. The same is also the case with "druggies," who are secretive and evasive. Somehow both species of maverick know how to put their best feet forward at job interviews before they trip over them in the field.

Legal defense of these testing requirements is tricky indeed. Where there is a clear-cut justification that public safety is at stake—employees in a nuclear power plant or railroad engineers—there isn't much quibbling. What rationale can you or your legal department come up with for the testing of your free-spirited mavericks? You're dealing with both a business and a moral issue which must be addressed by your company and your industry. To a certain extent we *are* our brother's keepers. It's part of the Code of the Old West.

Decision Time: Pick Your Winners and Cut Your Losses

The moment of truth has finally arrived—it's time to make your hiring decision. Whom will you select and why? Which finalist will you put your brand on as your next sales superstar? Everything that you've done until now is meaningless if you don't make a timely hiring decision. It's high time to pick your winners and cut your losses. Decisiveness is as important here as it is in other leadership situations. Yet each sales manager personality type approaches this task in a purely subjective manner.

Power Boss/Commander Selection Bias

"This is the marines! We're looking for a few good men who can make the grade." Will *he* hire a woman? Are you kidding? Not if he can help it! This is a he-man's outfit. He knows that a woman's place is in the home, baking cookies—certainly not selling. Will *she* hire a man? Why not? A female power boss/commander is very democratic about her harassment policies—anyone will do, at any time! She will most likely have a male secretary or assistant whom she can dominate. Will *either* of them hire an avoider/abdicator applicant? "Certainly not! Any wimp with such a weak handshake couldn't sell their way out of a wet paper bag! Did you see that creep? He wouldn't even look me in the eye and mumbled most of the time during the interview. How he ever got through screening, I'll never know."

Sometimes power bosses get stuck with avoider sales reps because nobody else answered their want ads, or they inherited them with the territory. Power bosses don't mind seeing these "weaklings" jump or run for cover whenever the PB/C has an emotional outburst. It's good for the power boss ego.

What about an affiliator/pleaser salesperson? "That lazy rascal! All he ever does is make excuses about the 'big order' that's coming and brag about all the great customer contacts he has out there in the field. He likes my war stories and laughs at all my jokes, so he can't be all bad." Pleasers are nice to have around the ranch because they know how to please the boss, stroke his or her ego, and serve as a punching bag on appropriate occasions. These cheerleader types smooth over any dissension in the ranks caused by the power boss's abrasive leadership style and thereby help to keep turnover down. Without them, there might be a mutiny every other week.

Will a power boss ever hire an achiever/technician salesperson? You bet your life that he or she will! Who else is going to do all the dirty work? Certainly not the PB/C, he or she has much more important things to do than mess around with a lot of stupid reports and paperwork. Avoiders and manipulators are also welcome to those chores.

What about a fellow power boss/commander salesperson? No question about it, he or she would be the power boss's kind of maverick: assertive and decisive with a strong action orientation. Their "welcome aboard" speech would be brief but to the point. "Just don't forget who the boss is, and we're going to get along just fine. Now go out there and kick some butt."

A manipulator/facilitator salesperson would come on to a power boss like gangbusters but would back down when necessary and would be willing to relieve that executive of his or her administrative duties and stroke his or her ego as necessary. Because of the manipulator's chameleon-like quality, these mavericks can take on the persona of a junior power boss, which is very acceptable to the big power boss ego.

Affiliator/Pleaser Selection Bias

"This is a real fun place to work. Everyone is super—like a warm and cozy country club atmosphere. I love my job, I love my customers, and I dearly love my company." Will this kind of sales manager ever hire a power boss/commander? What a foolish question. All those hardheads ever do is rock the boat and upset relationships. They would rather have those icky avoider/abdicator subordinates rather than have to deal with those troublemakers. Turn a couple of those lunatics loose, and they'll destroy your organization in nothing flat, but the avoiders are a horse of a different color. "Although I can't stand the way those sadsacks dress or their messy desks, they do handle all the nitty-gritty paperwork that I hate. They also take a lot of abuse from angry customers without quitting, so I guess that I can tolerate 'em."

Affiliator sales managers find achiever reps both boring and predictable, but they do bring in the business and get their paperwork done on time. Frequently, affiliators are compelled to come to the achiever for help on technical matters and other customer problems.

Affiliators are frequently taken in by a manipulator/facilitator's charm, convinced that this maverick is a fellow affiliator/pleaser and therefore one of the good old boys or gals.

Whom do you think that this free-spirited sales manager would prefer to hire above all others? You bet your boots—it would be another people pleaser just like himself or herself. This would seem to be the ideal match for both of them. They would have so much fun on the job, sitting around the ranch all day long drinking coffee and swapping war stories, or riding the range together, making joint calls where they could "press the flesh" with all of those great customers. They'd have a ball. "God love 'em. I wish I had a hundred more, just like them," sighs an affiliator/pleaser boss.

"That's just the trouble," sighs a disgruntled achiever/technician boss. "I've already got *five* hundred and wish that I only had *one* hundred, just like 'em!"

Achiever/Technician Selection Bias

There is no way that this kind of sales manager would ever hire an affiliator/pleaser sales candidate. "I've got enough flakes and BS artists in my organization right now. What do I need another lazy bum like this for? Oh yes, sometimes they get lucky and stumble across some gossip that we can cash in on and are good at hand holding, but who can stand their flashy clothes and cornball jokes?"

Will he or she hire a power boss? Yes, particularly if there are some really tough assignments coming up or the company is in a cold-calling mode. The PB/C's lack of a database is extremely disconcerting to achievers, but PB/Cs are great troubleshooters and know how to get things moving, both in the office and out in the field.

What about hiring avoider/abdicators? Sure, someone's got to handle routine matters, write the sales manual, and do research. They are loyal, dedicated, and dependable and love routine, and hate change. You can count on them to be at the same place at the same time each month, and established accounts love 'em.

You know that achiever/technician sales managers are going to hire other technically oriented mavericks who are either manipulator/ facilitators or fellow achievers. Because they are relatively insensitive to people, they cannot distinguish between the two personality types. Both use data to make decisions, are good at time and territory management, and respond favorably to a challenge.

Avoider/Abdicator Selection Bias

Whoever would give this sales manager personality type the least amount of hassle would be hired—after due deliberation, of course. No snap decisions here, only procrastination. Fellow avoiders and manipulators easily blend into this low-key category, but power bosses and affiliators should be avoided at all cost. The former is too loud and pushy, while the latter is too rowdy and rambunctious. Still, there are times when force and flamboyance are needed in a sales organization, but the avoider usually tries to duck those difficult customer encounters and company social events.

Achiever mavericks are preferable sales reps to the avoider because they are neat and well-organized, get their paperwork done on time, and can be counted upon to make quota. Sometimes, however, they get a little too big for their britches and can be a little bit too assertive for their own good. Manipulator mavericks play a supportive role and often relieve their avoider boss from tough assignments with deadlines, or from interpersonal human relations problems. Since a manipulator is not a perceived threat to the avoider boss, they seem to work well together.

Manipulator/Facilitator
Selection Bias

These savvy sales managers seek candidates with the capacity to grow and achieve—regardless of personality type—and who can interact effectively with peers, superiors, and customers. They want to meld these different attitudes, abilities, experiences, and viewpoints into a well-balanced team. They will orchestrate each unique maverick talent into a long-term and mutually beneficial situation. Although manipulator/

facilitator sales managers would secretly prefer having junior manipulators selling for them, they can build a successful sales organization with just about anyone who qualifies for membership. They know that anyone who is given proper training and guidance can become their "most valuable player."

How Do Salespeople Select Their Sales Managers?

The selection process is a two-way street whereby both parties select each other based on their own personality style and needs. True to their nature, mavericks select their sales managers on precisely the same basis that they are selected — namely through their own subjective bias and personal prejudices. They select the sales manager, the job, and the company in that order of preference.

A power boss maverick feels comfortable around other strong personalities, detests weaklings, tolerates achievers and affiliators, and is fooled by the manipulator. An avoider maverick fears the brash power boss, emulates achievers and manipulators, dislikes the noisy affiliator, but feels most comfortable with another avoider. An affiliator maverick also fears the power boss, is impatient with an avoider, doesn't understand or appreciate achievers or manipulators, and will prefer another affiliator. An achiever maverick is irritated by the busybody affiliator, the "smiler-and-filer" avoider, and the pugnacious power boss. He or she is delighted with manipulators and fellow achievers as possible leadership role models.

The manipulator maverick is a special case. He or she will work for any or all of the five psychological personality types but for different reasons. He or she will work for an avoider because the manipulator will have the avoider's job within a year. These subtle opportunists learn the business from achievers and all the gossip from their affiliator superiors. They know how to manage their power boss bosses and get what they want and perhaps ride up the organizational ladder on their coattails. A fellow manipulator is viewed as a superb role model who offers a fantastic learning experience in corporate chicanery. Their ambivalent relationship will continue as they rise to the top together.

Figure 7-1 illustrates who maverick sales candidates prefer to have as their sales managers and what would be their most consistent choice. If salespeople could select their own "ideal" bosses, they will choose to work for someone just like themselves. Therefore, the implications are

Maverick profile	Sales manager personality type					Best choice
	PB/C	A/P	A/A	A/T	M/F	
Power boss/ commander	✕				✕	M/F A/T
Affiliator/ pleaser		✕			✕	M/F A/T
Avoider/ abdicator			✕		✕	M/F A/T
Achiever/ technician			✕	✕		M/F A/P
Manipulator/ facilitator				✕	✕	M/F PB/C A/P A/A A/T

Figure 7-1. Maverick selection bias.

obvious—become a manipulator/facilitator sales manager, and *everyone* will want to work for you.

Should You Put the Offer in Writing?

Yup. A verbal agreement and a handshake are no longer good enough. If you don't put your job offer in writing, you could wind up shaking in your boots. Written employment agreements help avoid misunderstandings, demotivation, and possible litigation. Besides compensation and allowable travel and entertainment expenses, key areas to be clarified are

Territory coverage requirements

Handling of house accounts

Confidential company trade secrets and customer lists

Trade show responsibilities

Administrative duties

Termination of employment

I recommend annual contracts for *all* of your mavericks which clearly spell out the terms and conditions of employment as well as *mutually agreed-upon sales goals*. Besides having a signed legal document that will stand up in court, you have a *control device* which can help you monitor and measure maverick performance throughout the year. It is also a splendid appraisal tool. Written contracts take the guesswork and emotion out of the annual review session and provide you with a grand opportunity to motivate your mavericks to reach their full selling potential.

Postdecision Follow-Up

As soon as your preferred candidate has accepted your job offer, the other contenders should be immediately contacted. Do this by letter, but refrain from giving your reasons for rejecting them, as this could come back to haunt you later on in court. Always be courteous and polite to all applicants; you are a professional sales manager. It's part of the Code of the Old West.

Have your boss—or, preferably, the company president—write a "welcome aboard" letter to your new hiree. It will start the recognition process off on the right foot and also reassure this maverick that he or she selected the right company. After all, they had other employment opportunities to choose from. A personal, handwritten note from you will have a similar motivational impact.

Are You Ready for the New Reps?

Whether you hire a group of full-time company salespeople or independent sales reps, you must make sure *beforehand* that the various support systems in your organization are firmly in place. For example, do you have a structured indoctrination and orientation program designed to assimilate your new mavericks into the company? Are there enough staff people available to answer all the questions that enthusiastic new reps can throw at them? If not, they will quickly lose that enthusiasm and become demotivated.

Are your firm's engineering, production, and other departments prepared to back up these new salespeople? Technical questions, demands for expediting, quotations, and delivery requests will increase dramatically as your new mavericks swing into action.

Will marketing, order processing, and payroll departments provide prompt commission payments, product deliveries, and full-scale advertising and sales promotional programs to back them up in the field? Can the home office supply catalogues, sales literature, engineering data sheets, direct-mail pieces, and product samples fast enough to keep your sales reps in high gear?

Finally, do you have a well-planned sales training program available to educate these newcomers? These are some of the components of a well-organized and internally supported sales force. Obviously some of these elements are beyond your control, but they all affect your ability to hire and retain good salespeople.

Chapter 7 Roundup

Your interviewing sessions have narrowed the field to a few finalists. You've checked their references, administered appropriate tests, interviewed their spouses, and ultimately made a hiring decision. You've put the offer in writing, received an acceptance, and alerted your organization to prepare for the new maverick's arrival. Your job appears to be done for now, but recruiting is an ongoing process for dynamic sales organizations. You will always be on the lookout for new talent. Sir Arthur Conan Doyle put it perfectly: "Mediocrity knows nothing higher than itself, but talent instantly recognizes genius." That must be your attitude throughout the entire selection process. You never know when your next future superstar will appear on the selling scene. It's always high noon at the hiring corral.

PART 3
Motivation of Staff and Self

Never tell people how *to do things. Tell them* what *to do and they will surprise you with their ingenuity.*

GEORGE S. PATTON

8

Breaking In
the New Mavericks

*The world breaks everyone and afterward
many are strong at the broken places.*
ERNEST HEMINGWAY

Introduction to Orientation
and Training

The big recruiting roundup is over, and you've lassoed a new herd of mavericks for your corral. Now it's time to break in these newcomers so that they will become strong in *every* place. You will guide them through a series of internal company programs that begin with orientation and conclude with sales training. This chapter deals with those structured activities that are designed to strengthen their selling sinews.

Inside Indoctrination:
Learning the Ropes

All of the time, money, and effort which you expended in the selection process can be completely nullified by a poor indoctrination program. You've got to put your official brand on these new employees before they are ready to sell your company's products or services. New mavericks who are formally assimilated into a firm learn the ropes quicker and are able to contribute sooner, perform more effectively, and stay longer than greenhorns whose indoctrination was loose, disorganized, or nonexistent.

Before they report for work, order their business cards, and send them a corporate orientation booklet which covers all the details of the job. Your human resources department should also send them information on company policy, procedures, and compensation. New mavericks, like anyone else, are threatened by change and are somewhat ill-at-ease in a new working environment. You want them to feel welcome and comfortable so that their learning curve can be shortened.

Orientation Objectives and Methods

In addition to making these new employees feel welcome and at ease, you want them to absorb everything possible to start performing their selling jobs. This includes understanding what you and the company expect of them in terms of work performance and behavior as well as where and to whom to go for help within the organization.

Most orientation programs fall within the domain of the human resources department, but your direct involvement will make a lasting impression on your new reps. Among other things, it will give them insights into your leadership style and method of operation. As mentioned in Chap. 7, before they officially check in, write them a "welcome aboard" letter, and invite them to an informal social gathering—or your next sales meeting—where they can meet the rest of the team. Then circulate an information sheet on each new maverick that indicates his or her rank, position, and location in your sales organization. This way, nobody gets his or her nose out of joint.

A private chat with each new rep precedes the group introductory meeting. You prime them for the group session and give them their business cards. This is another opportunity for you to clarify and confirm their job responsibilities and accountabilities while communicating your high expectations and performance standards. After answering any questions, you personally conduct them to the meeting and introduce them to their fellow comrades in arms. This procedure will clarify role relationships and avoid possible misunderstandings which could affect team morale and job performance later on.

Length and Coverage of Your Orientation Program

Depending upon the needs of your organization and the experience level of your new sales reps, your program could last from a few days to a couple of weeks. Since this is a *doing* activity, most of the leadership of the indoctrination course can be delegated to other functional department heads. The following are examples listed by subject matter.

Topic	Discussion leader
1. Corporate overview	Human resources director
2. Mission statement	Executive vice president
3. Payroll and benefits	Human resources director
4. Operations	Vice president of production and/or manufacturing
5. Safety	Plant safety director
6. Credit policies	Chief financial officer
7. Accounting practices	Vice president of accounting
8. Sales administration	Sales administrator
9. Proposal preparation	Sales administrator
10. Marketing strategy	Vice president of marketing
11. Advertising and sales promotion	Director of advertising
12. District sales activities	District sales manager

Set reasonable home study and reading assignments so that the new reps won't get information overload. Allow enough time in your course for evaluation and review. You want to be sure that this educational vaccination will "take." These intensive activities should go a long way toward aligning new employee expectations with actual job responsibilities. When it's all over (including any training courses, as discussed below), they "graduate." Give them each a certificate of completion of the company orientation program—the Silver Bullet Award. Then throw a graduation party in their honor. This kind of recognition will go a long ways toward building positive leader-member relations.

The Case for Inside Training

Once the right rookies are in place and the appropriate relationships established, you can now turn your attention to their training and development needs. Before you turn these new recruits loose on the unsuspecting public, they should be given a crash course in professional selling. The length and breadth of your inside training program will vary according to the urgency of filling your open territories, the complexity of your product line or service package, and the intellectual capacity of your trainees.

No one should be sent out into the field who is not fully prepared to sell. Yet some misguided sales "manglers" want their new sales reps to produce orders *before* they will invest any training funds in them. This is the so-called Czarist Syndrome of Sales Management and was rumored to have been started by his chief bean counter.

The Czarist Syndrome of Sales Management

During the Russo-Japanese War, the Russian czar prepared his troops for battle in the following manner: The first wave of charging infantrymen was given rifles, the second wave was provided with clubs, but the third wave was given nothing but good wishes. They were supposed to pick up the weapons from their fallen comrades and then continue the attack.

If you were recruited into that army, which wave would you choose? That's exactly how rookie salespeople feel when they are sent into the field without adequate tools to do their jobs. That's no way to break in a new maverick; it sure will burn them right out of the business.

Denying the training and support systems which every jittery newcomer needs to get started in selling is a short-sighted and counterproductive view of the sales team–building process. New reps are entitled to all of the help and tangible support that you and your organization can provide. Success in selling is inversely related to a salesperson's FUD factor—Fear, Uncertainty, and Doubt—which they experience every day on the firing line. Because selling will always be a problem if it is not learned as a procedure, it is mandatory that selling skills—as well as product knowledge—be emphasized in your training programs. Without adequate preparation, new salespeople will surely fail in the field—just as the ill-equipped and poorly trained Russian soldiers did.

Training Sequence

The first phase of your sales training program should have occurred during the second selection interview. When you were "selling" qualified applicants on the job opportunity, you gave them product literature and discussed the benefits of your product line or service package. The orientation phase continued the training process by acquainting new employees with company background, corporate goals and philosophies, management structure, and operations. Now, sales training focuses on product knowledge and selling skills development. Topical areas to be covered and their sequential order are determined by a number of significant factors.

Determining Sales Training Needs

In assessing the training requirements for your organization, you must consider the maturity and selling experience levels of your individual mavericks as well as their field working conditions and your high standards of job performance. Obviously, there is a vast difference between the training needs of rookies and those of seasoned veterans. In both cases, however, effective sales training courses should provide them with product knowledge and selling skills which they are currently lacking but need to perform their jobs successfully. If they fail—and many will—you've got to ask yourself if *you* failed to provide them with all of the aid and support that they needed to do the job. These are some of *your* most important job responsibilities.

Needs Analysis First

Before you establish your training program, it is essential that both you and your staff understand its purpose, agree upon objectives, and be able to ascertain when desired performance is being done well and why. Input from your firm's human resources department and your more experienced senior sales executives would be most welcome. Together, you must analyze your staff's sales training needs and then establish priorities so that those areas of the highest performance improvement payout are done first. Differentiate between need-to-know and nice-to-know topics.

Although the primary objective of sales training is to increase order productivity and job satisfaction, other valid goals include improved staff morale, lowered turnover, reduced selling costs, more efficient time and territory management, and improved customer relations. Sales training objectives are inherently motivational because of the personal recognition factor, can influence long-term behavioral change, and provide an objective basis for measuring job performance.

What Skills Should Be Emphasized?

The need for formal training increases with the technical complexity of your product or service, variety of distribution, and sophistication

level of your clientele. Evaluate the maturity and experiential levels of your individual mavericks and then perform a difficulty analysis. These are the challenges and obstacles that your reps are en-
countering in the field. Some sales terrains are more treacherous
than others, but you should know this wilderness trail from your
own outrider days. Identifying these "difficulties" will enable you to
design the appropriate training modules to help your mavericks
prevail.

Subjects which are most frequently emphasized during inside sales-training programs include the following:

1. Planning and organizing available resources
2. The psychology of selling
3. Developing a sales call plan
4. Classifying current customers on a gross-sales and profitable-volume basis
5. Managing time and territory effectively
6. Routing sales calls on an efficient basis
7. Improving prospecting methods
8. Sizing up customer personality types
9. Translating product features into buyer benefits
10. Using the telephone more effectively
11. Dynamic sales presentation techniques
12. Handling objections and closing the sale
13. Aspects of customer service and follow-through
14. Administrative details (proposal preparation, credit checks, filling out the
    order form, call reports, expense forms, office procedures, etc.)
15. Setting goals and sales forecasting

Based upon your own unique selling situation and the needs of your
salespeople, you will select those skills that you want to develop or improve. Ascertain the most educationally sound and practical method to
communicate these needed skills and desired knowledge. Then determine the sequence of these skill-building modules and the time allocations for each skill and knowledge deficiency. A decision should now be
made regarding the number of days needed to teach the required skills
and the sequential timing of each segment. After determining the training location and who will do the training, you can order the appropriate
audiovisual equipment and programmed learning materials. Figure 8-1
gives you a suggested format for training new sales reps, and Fig. 8-2
does the same for experienced mavericks. In both cases you should spice
up the lingo and use verbal-proof stories to make each dose of training
more palatable.

Figure **8-1**. Suggested training program for new mavericks.

I. Introduction
   A. Welcome aboard
   B. Course content and objectives
   C. Overview of the company
      1. Chain of command
      2. Products, services, policies, and procedures

II. Program format
   A. What is professional selling?
   B. The psychology of selling
   C. Attributes of successful salespeople — Case Study
   D. How to listen actively
   E. Prospecting — sales development
      1. Separating suspects from prospects
      2. Resources for finding new prospects
      3. The qualifying process
   F. Precall planning
      1. New account strategy
      2. Sales development versus sales maintenance
   G. What motivates people to buy?
      1. Buyer needs and buying motives
      2. Consumer buying behavior
   H. Figuring out the buyer
      1. You and the customer grid
      2. Psychological customer profiling
      3. Coping behavior — Case Study
   I. The selling process — persuasive communications
      1. Different types of sales presentations
      2. Proper sequencing of your sales pitch
      3. Buyer feedback allowances
      4. Recognizing cues to adapt your presentation
      5. Videotaped role playing
   J. Handling objections
      1. Basic categories of objections
      2. Difference between excuses and objections
      3. Overcoming objections with finesse
      4. Videotape feedback for role playing situations
   K. Closing the sale
      1. Purchase commitment sensitivity
      2. Variety of effective closes
      3. Videotape role playing situations

(Continued)

Figure 8-1. Suggested training program for new mavericks. *(Continued)*

>   L. Following through with the customer
>   1. Postsales service
>   2. Handling problems and complaints
>   3. Obtaining leads and referrals
>   M. Summary
>   1. Selling skills practice
>   2. Videotaping and group critique
>
> III. Conclusion
>   A. Inspirational film
>   B. Development of territorial objectives
>   C. Evaluation of course (usually in writing)
>   D. Adjournment

Who Should Do the Training?

Although your firm's human resources department usually plays a dominant role in the design and delivery of most employee training programs, your involvement in sales training is crucial to your relationship with your new mavericks. Let them benefit from your knowledge and front-line selling experience. You're the leader of the herd, and your example inside the classroom will spur your rookies on to grand achievements out on the range.

Because of limitations on time, geography, and your attention span, most of the training activities can be delegated to your qualified regional sales managers, district managers, and senior sales reps who possess teaching ability. Some organizations have full-time company sales trainers, who specialize in this important activity. If you are not fortunate enough to have these training experts on your staff, you can either engage the services of an outside sales training consultant, delegate to the sales executives previously mentioned, or do it yourself.

Delegation of this crucial management function is highly motivational to those who are called upon to lead the various segments of the course. Affiliator/pleasers and power boss/commanders seize every opportunity to perform. They love to show off and strut their stuff in public. Avoider/abdicators certainly know their subject matter well enough but tend to overprepare and are reluctant to appear in front of *any* group of people. Achiever/technicians also overprepare and tend to emphasize the technical side of each topic and are guilty of information overkill. What else could be more important? Manipulator/facilitators do a superb job and can be counted upon to pitch in with both the design and

Figure 8-2. Suggested training program for experienced mavericks.

I. Introduction
  A. Course content and objectives
  B. Review of product lines or service package
     1. Best-sellers and profit leaders
     2. New products and "dogs"
     3. Technical aspects—"hands on" session

II. Program format
  A. Problem-solving selling
     1. Market linkage and consultative selling
     2. Value-added selling
     3. Salesperson as marketing manager of his or her sales territory
     4. Developing your sales presentation
        a. Translating product and/or service features into buyer benefits
        b. Product line or service package—Case Study
  B. The true cost and value of your time in relation to actual customer contact time
     1. How do most sales reps spend their time?
     2. Notorious time-management traps
     3. How much is your time worth? Where are you spending it?
     4. When to ask for a raise or make up your résumé
  C. Plan and manage your selling efforts
     1. Account profitability and territorial analysis
     2. Prospecting and time management
     3. Determining your sales call objectives
     4. Routing sales trips on a cost-effective basis
     5. Developing a sales call plan
     6. Account classification—Case Study
  D. Telephone solicitation techniques
     1. Use of the telephone as a programming tool
     2. Obtain and confirm appointments
     3. The "Mr. Davis" call
     4. Closing orders and increasing face-to-face selling time
     5. Advantages and disadvantages of telemarketing
  E. The seven psychological steps to the sale
     1. Opening the sales interview

(Continued)

Figure 8-2. Suggested training program for experienced mavericks. *(Continued)*

    2. The qualification
    3. Obtaining appropriate information
    4. Establishing your customer's criteria for buying
    5. Selling benefits and solutions
    6. The parallel technique of selling
    7. Videotape role playing and critique

F. The customer buying center concept
    1. Who are the decision makers and influencers?
    2. Group selling reconnaissance and presentations
    3. Selling to and through committees
    4. Planning your individual account selling strategy

G. Overcoming objections
    1. Classifying objections
    2. Prehandling objections
    3. Coping with competition
    4. Summarizing for agreement (before closing)
    5. Videotape role playing and feedback

H. Closing the sale
    1. Your closing attitude
    2. Verbal and nonverbal closing cues
    3. Listening skills and qualifying questions
    4. Buttoning up the sale and following through
    5. Obtaining leads and referrals

III. Conclusion

A. Self-image psychology
    1. *Psycho-Cybernetics.* These are techniques for building self-confidence and source credibility.
    2. *Transactional analysis* and other interpersonal communications theories. Insight into the way people establish relationships and relate to each other is a vital part of the persuasion process.
    3. *The influence of fear on salespeople.* This subject speaks for itself.

B. Goal-setting exercise

C. Motivational conclusion and send-off

presentation of materials. They are splendid classroom facilitators and deliver a balanced blend of technical and nontechnical data.

In addition to outside training firms and consultants, other available training resources include printed materials, audiovisual programs, guest speakers, and outside courses and seminars. *A word of caution:* When in-house company staff or outside resource people are used to train sales reps, credibility is sometimes missing. George Bernard Shaw put it aptly: "He who can, does. He who cannot, teaches." That's the maverick view of the educational process and perhaps of most sales training in general. If the instructor has never sold anything before, he or she will have a tough time selling knowledge and ideas in the classroom to these tough hombres. They know that you can no more teach a subject that you don't know than lead people to a place you've never been. The power bosses in the group will have that instructor for lunch the very first day.

Where Should the Sales Training Be Done?

Sales training—like recruiting—is a continuous process and therefore can occur at any time or place, provided that the trainer has prepared beforehand. Consider this variety of locations:

1. The centralized company training facility
2. Home office or field sales office conference room
3. A local company branch office
4. Company plant locations
5. A hotel or motel meeting room
6. An airport terminal conference room
7. A restaurant or a private club
8. A customer's place of business
9. Your ranch or theirs
10. Your automobile or theirs

Although a number of these locations are mainly used for outside training and coaching in the field, the possibilities are endless. Use your imagination. Napoleon Bonaparte once said that "imagination rules the world." An alert sales manager finds every opportunity to teach selling skills to his or her mavericks. It also keeps the teacher sharp.

Sales Training Techniques That Pay Off

There are essentially two main sales training techniques: nonpartici-pative and participative. Each has inherent advantages and limitations which you should evaluate before adopting either of them. A combination of the two is recommended for best overall results.

Nonparticipative Techniques

Nonparticipative methods don't require trainees to actively respond to instructor input or other stimuli. They are utilized for the infusion of theoretical information. There are basically four kinds of nonparticipatory sales training techniques.

   1. *Lecture.*   This is what most college professors, avoider/abdicators, and some achiever/technicians favor. Power boss/commanders are also big on this method because they are center stage and have complete control of their audience plus it's good for their ego. This method can be effective if you use range vernacular while appealing to your audi-ence's self-interest. Unfortunately, this is the *weakest* method of com-municating knowledge and information because there is no provision for feedback. It is similar to a maverick's "canned pitch" sales presenta-tion in the field before a dozing customer who is faking interest. There is no listener involvement, and you are never really sure if you have their attention. Most mavericks have mastered the art of smiling blandly at an instructor, mechanically nodding their heads in apparent agree-ment, while mentally planning their weekend agenda. If you find them squirming in their seats and doing a lot of yawning, then you know that you've been beating your gums too long.

   2. *Demonstrations.*   These are marginally better than lectures be-cause they introduce an element of drama into the classroom. Although they illustrate "how to" techniques and functional product and/or ser-vice features, there is still no trainee involvement or feedback. Achiever/technicians, avoider/abdicators, and other "techies" love this method of instruction because they can demonstrate how smart *they* are. Therefore, judicious use of this technique is recommended. Like in sell-ing, the more listener involvement in training, the better.

   3. *Movies, slide presentations, and other audiovisual materials.*   These training techniques utilize sound, color, and motion but also do not allow for any viewer feedback. That's why they are the favorite teaching meth-ods of avoider/abdicator sales managers. All they have to do is plug in the

projector, start the tape player, and retreat to the rear of the room. While lurking in the darkness, all they have left to do in this tough teaching assignment is to hit the "change slide" button whenever they hear the beep on the tape machine. They don't have to talk, look at anyone, or answer any nit-picky questions. They hope that the equipment will jam so that the day's training session will get called off altogether.

Achiever/technicians and manipulator/facilitators make more creative use of these electronic media and turn them into truly effective learning devices. They stop these audiovisual presentations and insert short, thought-provoking comments and minilectures that elicit individual and group responses. Sometimes they even spring a popquiz on their participants after the conclusion of the film.

A word of caution: Never show a film immediately after the lunch hour, unless you want your audience to catch up on their sleep. That's the toughest instructional time for both teacher and student because the human digestive process is competing for attention. It's best to get your audience up on their feet or involved with some kind of participative exercise. The best time slots for films are very early in the morning, just *before* noon, or at the end of the afternoon session.

---

4. *Reading assignments and dramatic presentations.* These can work splendidly if combined in an imaginative way. You can give the group a reading assignment and ask trainees to either write up reports or take tests to measure their understanding. By having them make dramatic presentations or role-play the material from the assigned readings, you are combining this nonparticipatory technique (reading) with participatory techniques (dramatizations and role-playing) in a most effective manner.

Participative Techniques That Stimulate

Participative methods require active involvement by the class. They are action-oriented and stimulate audience feedback and involvement in the learning process. Since mavericks are action-oriented doers by nature, they find participative learning techniques most stimulating.

The earliest recorded usage of this teaching technique was in ancient Greece by that famous philosopher maverick, Socrates, who taught by indirection. He challenged his students' opinions and asked them questions about their answers. Through these continuous probes, he was able to show them how inadequate their opinions and assumptions really were and opened their minds to real learning. By going beyond biased opinion and narrow assumption, he helped them to search out essential meanings and the truth.

Isn't this Socratic method the same technique that you use in field selling situations as well as in classroom training? A consultative salesperson uses this method when a skeptical prospect is unaware of the existence of an urgent problem or need. Through the use of indirection— questions, probes, and conditioned responses—the alert maverick makes her or his buyer aware of the magnitude of the operational problem that their product or service can solve, and then guides that buyer to an applicable solution. Range riders call this technique, "giving your prospects a headache, before you give them an aspirin." In the field, the aspirin is your product or service, while in the training classroom, it's knowledge and truth. (Be careful that your long-windedness doesn't give each customer *earaches*.)

Of all the participative training techniques available, the most frequently used are the role play and critique, buzz groups, case studies, group discussions, roundtables, and panel discussions. Any method that you can use to get group and individual involvement and stimulate feedback is worth trying. Make sure that you have previously established a positive and supportive atmosphere. Your attitude must be that there are no stupid questions, and we're all in this cattle drive together, so let's help each other out whenever we can. There shouldn't be any cabin fever in your training bunkhouse.

How Each Personality Type Applies These Techniques

Avoider/abdicator sales managers feel threatened by group exposure in the classroom and feel speechless and somewhat inadequate when put on the spot with student questions. They usually delegate—by default— this odious assignment to others and abdicate this responsibility completely. Power boss/commanders are too impatient with all those stupid questions that those imbecile trainees always ask. They would also like to get out of this dumb duty.

Achiever/technicians also think that trainees are brain-dead, but they do a decent job of leading participatory sessions. They are sticklers for starting and ending on time—and that includes class discussions. Affiliator-pleasers are definitely in their element in a classroom. They are personally stimulated by group activities and relish the feeling of finding new friends and influencing people. By imparting their selling knowledge, these happy executives are "pleasing" yet another generation of potential admirers and feel a part of their future successes. They have a great sense of humor and are excellent at building relationships but tend to wander astray from the agenda to tell one of their favorite homespun yarns.

Manipulator/facilitators are the very best teachers of them all. They orchestrate a classroom environment where everyone is stimulated to learn, through an apt combination of participatory and nonpartici-patory techniques that have just the right blend of style and substance. This is also an opportunity to spot the "comers" in the crowd and start planning their careers. If they play their cards right, one of them can become a protégé.

How Long Should Sales Training Last?

To do a decent job, six weeks to six months of intensive training is re-quired. An effective training course picks up from where your orienta-tion and indoctrination programs leave off. You are the best judge of the time required to break in your new mavericks. One of the key ques-tions for you to consider is Which is easier to teach, product and/or ser-vice knowledge or selling skills? If you've hired a lot of technically ori-ented ranch hands, you should focus on developing their human skills and conceptual skills. Classroom instruction should emphasize persua-sive interpersonal communication and selling techniques. When you are satisfied that enough progress has been made in these areas, you should have them start in the customer service department so that they can learn your business from your client's perspective.

Trainees with nontechnical backgrounds but with good human skills should be given a heavy dose of product and/or service knowledge in addition to selling skills. Their conceptual skills should be tested and stretched to a satisfactory level. After the formalized sales training course is over, they should spend time in the engineering and produc-tion departments so that they can learn about the technical capabilities of your company and its products and services. It will also give them a conceptual view of the business.

If you can get both kinds of maverick trainees to perceive that their firm's prod-ucts and services are *tools that solve client problems* and that they are selling *so-lutions* and not "pushing product," they will be able to make the difficult tran-sition from raw recruits to professional salespeople more easily.

The Silver Bullet Award

Upon completion of your sales training course, everyone is invited to a good old-fashioned chuck wagon dinner party. During this celebration, each graduate is given the Silver Bullet Award which symbolizes that they are now equipped with the ammunition they need to get the job done in the field. Now these new mavericks must "earn their spurs." You've done your job; now it's time for them to do theirs. They've got to start drumming up some business to earn their keep.

Sales Manager as Supertrainer

A good training program reinforces the attitude that a professional salesperson can never achieve perfection. The same is also true about sales managers who do the training. New educational techniques are constantly being developed by innovative trainers and creative sales managers. One way to keep yourself up to date on the latest evolutions in this dynamic field is to join such professional organizations as the National Society of Sales Training Executives, the American Society for Training and Development, and the Sales & Marketing Executives Club in your local area. Periodic contact with other sales managers and professional sales training consultants will keep you abreast of current events in the training world and stimulate some new ideas of your own on the subject.

Make It a Mission—Get Obsessed

You should also read every new book and published article on selling, sales training, leadership, and sales management. Attend every seminar offered on these subjects, especially those educational workshops which are sponsored by professional organizations, like the American Management Association, and consulting firms in your industry. Where possible, attend university extension courses on sales management and train-the-trainer programs. Even teaching a course in professional selling at a local junior college or university will keep you in shape. Finally, you should have a current library of audio- and videocassettes on selling techniques that you can listen to during "drive time" and perhaps utilize in your next training session.

These are some of the ways that you can strive for perfection as a developer of salespeople. It is consistent with that great American tradition as noted by Alexis de Tocqueville more than a century ago.

> They [the Americans] have all a lively faith in the perfectibility of man, they judge the diffusion of knowledge must necessarily be advantageous, and the consequences of ignorance fatal; they all consider society as a body in a state of improvement, humanity as a changing scene, in which nothing is, or ought to be, permanent; and they admit that what appears to them today to be good, may be superseded by something better tomorrow.

Chapter 8 Roundup

Breaking in your new mavericks and teaching them the ropes can be a pretty tricky proposition. Horse sense suggests that you make them feel at home in their new company corral. You can accomplish this through a dynamite orientation and indoctrination program. Your inside training program should emphasize products and/or services and company knowledge along with selling skills development.

Teach these boisterous buckaroos all the tricks of the trade so that they can go out into their far-flung territories and start bagging some accounts. Upon completion of this journey of learning, a certificate of graduation—the Silver Bullet Award—is presented to each new outrider. Then turn 'em loose, and hope for the best. It's high time for them to start earning their spurs on the selling range while you sharpen your role as sales trainer and slick spinner of educational yarns.

9

Riding Shotgun with Your Mavericks

Good counselors lack no clients.
WILLIAM SHAKESPEARE

Introduction to Outside Training

Riding shotgun in the field with your mavericks means cashing in on your hiring and training investment. It is the directing and controlling phase of sales management. This chapter covers those activities involved in the outside training, coaching, and counseling of your salespeople. They have just finished their inside indoctrination and sales training programs and are raring to go. Sir Francis Bacon said that "knowledge is power," but knowledge is useless unless profitably applied. All the silver bullets in the world won't mean diddly unless your new reps can close orders. Timely field follow-up will pay off handsomely for both you and them in terms of organizational goals, morale, and new-employee retention.

The Benefits of Outside Training

Here is a golden opportunity for you to assert your leadership in the field and share your unique selling experience with both rookies and old pros. Riding tall in the saddle, you can direct field selling operations where the action is. Under these combat conditions you can really get to know your reps better and open up the lines of interpersonal communication. Outside training is by far the most effective means of teaching sales skills because you are operating under actual field selling conditions. If your new mavericks screw up, they've had it. Customers aren't nearly as forgiving as training instructors. One false move, and your rookie is history. Your task is to minimize their errors, build up their confidence, and help them translate classroom theory into profitable performance.

When Should the Outside Training Begin?

Give your newcomers some space. Turn 'em loose to roam the range with the other wild animals. Let them get their feet wet and take their lumps before you ride to the rescue. After a few weeks of hard knocks, rejection, and outright blunders, they will be more receptive to your first visit on their turf. Don't just pop in on them; give your new mavericks the courtesy of sufficient advance notice. Call them up on the telephone at least two weeks *before* you intend to ride shotgun with them, and then establish:

1. *The exact dates and number of days you want to work with them, so as to avoid any schedule conflicts.*

2. *That you want to make sales calls together on prospects who are* not *presently using your firm's products and services or are only using them on a limited basis.*   You state that this is going to be a working session and not merely a "goodwill" tour of their territory.

3. *Which types of joint calls you would like to make together and why.*   (This applies only if your product or service involves multiple buying influences or decision makers.)

4. *The kinds of samples, sales props, or visual aids that you will be bringing along with you and those which you expect them to have available.*   A well-known manufacturer of commercial refrigerators and freezers required all of its salespeople to lug around a 30-pound door sample that showed off its stainless steel construction, polyurethane insulation, and sturdy glass paneling. Dealers would jokingly complain that they were "strong-armed" into buying from those muscle-bound reps. Another example of Darwin's theory—survival of the fittest—as applied to modern selling!

5. *That your salesperson will set up calls with customers in a specific account classification or geographic area.* Then, together you ride full tilt.

Riding Shotgun in the Field

Be positive, enthusiastic, and reassuring when you arrive. New mavericks, despite their bluster and apparent nonchalance, are uptight and apprehensive whenever the boss appears in their territory, especially if they haven't written their first orders yet. Avoider/abdicators, in particular, always feel that they're going to be fired at any moment. Sometimes they are so nervous that they couldn't even give you their own names if you asked them. They are so jittery that if you tied cymbals to their knees you could probably hear them in the next county!

Therefore, your first task of the day is to relax your reps and state the objectives of your field visit. Chew the cud with them for awhile and emphasize that you are there to help them develop their skills by working together and sharing front-line selling experiences. You are following through on your firm's commitment to continuous training and development of their employees, and you are personally interested in their professional welfare and growth.

Precall Planning Activities

Once they know that they aren't going to be fired, your reps will relax and be more receptive to your next move, which is to get them to develop their planning capabilities. Before you make your first joint sales call, you should sit down with them to review their prospect list and ask the following probing questions:

1. *Where are we going and why? Is this really a worthwhile account? Are they worth our time and effort?*
   Get them to think in terms of account call priorities and time management.

2. *Who are we going to see and why? Does this executive have the authority to buy or influence a purchasing decision? Do we want to meet with more than one person, and how can we make it happen? Should a telephone call for an appointment be made beforehand?*
   Get your maverick to think in terms of account strategies and the efficient use of the telephone.

3. *What is the purpose of this call? Should this prospect visit have priority over other client calls to be made today? Why?*
Get them to think in terms of call objectives and where their most productive selling efforts should be directed.

4. *Where does this prospect company buy now? Why? Is there really any good reason why this firm should buy from us? What are those reasons?*
Get them to understand your firm's strength in the marketplace and identify competition.

5. *Are there any specific sales tools — samples, testimonial letters, audiovisuals, special materials — that you should use? Why? When? Where? How?*
Get your newcomer to think in terms of preparation and imaginative approaches to dramatize his or her sales presentation.

6. *Do you want to visit the plant or warehouse in addition to your prospect's office contacts? How will you make this happen? What obstacles are likely to arise? How will you overcome them?*
Get your rookies to think on their feet and plan ahead.

7. *Is this call an important step in the overall development of this prospective account? How? If not, why are we going there?*
Get your reps to think in terms of depth selling.

8. *What can you and I do on this joint call — outside of writing an order — that will lay the foundation for a long-term business relationship? Will you need technical support or other selling assistance?*
Get your mavericks to think in terms of long-term relationships rather than one-shot deals.

9. *When the customer visit is over, ask, "What was the bottom-line result of this sales call? Did we accomplish our call objectives? If not, why? If so, what were the most significant client reactions?"*
Get them to stay on track and control the visit.

10. *What must you do next with this account?*
Get them to think in terms of profitability and their home office support system.

These questions force a new rep to think through what he or she does before hitting the road and also encourages thoughtful postmortem sales call analysis. This kind of training improves planning capabilities and conditions your rep to set account goals and establish call priorities. It is the first step toward efficient time and territory management.

Now that you have your tenderfoot's head screwed on right, go over the tactics which you want used to accomplish your client call objectives. Together you review the types of questions which are to be used to open the visit, how the major selling points will be developed, and how to guide the prospects toward the ultimate call objectives. Closing techniques should then be discussed, practiced, and rehearsed in your presence. You can also drill them on other phases of selling until you're satisfied that they are ready for action. Don't ever let them buffalo you into thinking that they don't need your help.

First-Call Protocol

In the case of new mavericks, you will handle the first joint sales call and demonstrate in the prospect's office exactly what you had previously presented in the training classroom. By showing your rep what is the correct selling procedure, you will establish your credibility in his or her eyes. An order written in the field in front of a salesperson is worth a thousand sales training lectures in the office.

When this call concludes, your trainee gets into the driver's seat and takes over. He or she makes the next sales call while you take a back seat. And *back seat* is putting it mildly. Outside of the social part of the call, you will say absolutely nothing. If the prospect asks you a question, you defer to your salesperson. If either of them even looks in your direction while your rep is discussing the client's situation, you look away. This is your new maverick's show, and you do not want to intervene, even if he or she gets into trouble.

This is a learning-by-doing situation, and *patience* now becomes your middle name. You allow your new subordinate to struggle through this client call without any interference on your part so that you can observe the performance and assess his or her ability.

Even if he or she screws up the sale, do not jump in and try to save it. You must sit there quietly and bite your tongue — even if it kills you! If you can't resist this temptation — and few power bosses and achievers can — you will make that rookie a closing cripple for the rest of his or her life. Henceforth, he or she will become overly dependent upon you and be fearful of closing situations. Your impulsive act will rob your maverick of self-esteem and assertiveness. You will, in fact, have nullified all of your prior selection and training efforts by one rash action. Let that one order go, there will be others coming down the pike — probably more than good talent to recruit and train.

Power boss sales managers would rather save the order and cripple the rep because they *want* their salespeople to be dependent upon them so that they can control them. It also gratifies their ego to score bigtime in front of an admiring audience. Achiever sales managers have trouble delegating anything because they're so good at doing it themselves. Thus, at the first sign of trouble, they take over the sale. Both executive personalities are relatively insensitive to people, so they are unaware of the long-term damage that they are doing to their own sales organizations.

There are, of course, *exceptional situations* when you must take over the sale from a faltering rookie. For example, a very large order may be lost, there has been a serious misassessment of the prospect, or the newcomer is seriously embarrassing himself or herself and the company before a longtime customer. Then it's time to swing into action and see what you can salvage.

After-the-Call Critique

As soon as your rep-led sales call is over, grab some grub or a cup of coffee somewhere private, and review the performance in the prospect's office. This is the best time for appraising and correcting, because the events and impressions are still fresh in both of your minds. Sometimes it can even be done in the car, while you are driving to your next appointment.

The theme of your review session should be positive and constructive in nature. Compliment your rookie on those areas where he or she did well, and only criticize the most obvious blunders. If you try to correct many things at once, you may confuse or demoralize him or her. Power bosses usually come down too hard, while avoider and achiever sales managers nitpick 'em to death. Affiliators are too easy on their new reps and make excuses for their shortcomings. Manipulator/facilitator sales managers ask their trainees how they thought the sales call went and then have *them* review the particulars. Through the use of indirection — the Socratic method — they get them to see their mistakes and understand what they would do differently next time. Everything is positive and upbeat. Everybody has learned something constructive.

A word of caution: Never criticize a subordinate in front of a customer, or anyone else. Outside training is a private affair between you and your maverick, it's part of the Code of the Old West.

From that point on, you will alternate sales presentations until you have completed your tour of duty in the territory. Again, the training procedure is the same. You will observe your newcomer's selling behavior and give a critique immediately afterward, using the "sandwich approach": You begin by complimenting the rep on all of the good things that he or she did in the prospect's office and then hone in on the area that needs the most attention. You would then conclude on a positive and encouraging note. Sometimes it's a good idea to make the very next presentation and emphasize the area which you just reviewed with your trainee. That's when the real learning begins. You can see the light bulbs going on all over the place!

The Sink-or-Swim School of Hard Knocks

This is the favorite field initiation tactic used by direct-to-the-consumer product companies who sell items like Bibles, encyclopedias, brushes, storm doors, sidings, and pots and pans. New salespeople are taken out into the field and dumped off behind the enemy lines and allowed to fend for themselves. It's an updated version of Charles Darwin's survival-of-the-fittest theory because only the strongest mavericks survive this baptism of fire.

Power boss/commander and manipulator/facilitator sales managers in other selling arenas are also partial to this method because they like to see what kind of "stuff" these new recruits are made of. Their philosophy is both simple and direct: "Either they've got what it takes or they don't. It's better to find out sooner than later." Avoider/abdicators don't have the courage to do such a dastardly deed to a fellow human being, and affiliator/pleasers feel too sorry for the innocent victims to do it. Achiever/ technicians are also against the idea because statistics prove that this is a most inefficient method of breaking in new recruits and contributes directly to high employee turnover and shell shock. Here's how "dumping" works. You be the judge of its appropriateness for your sales organization.

The sales manager and the new trainee drive into the territory in separate cars, meet at a predetermined location—usually a restaurant or a coffee shop—and compare notes. After a brief planning session they depart in the sales manager's automobile for their destination—a lower middle class neighborhood. The sales manager knocks on the first door and uses the standard company door approach to gain entrance. He or she then qualifies this prospect family and proceeds to make the first sales presentation of the evening. The trainee relaxes and watches the boss perform. After they both depart, and regardless of the outcome of the sales call, the sales manager says to the trainee, "Now that wasn't so bad, was it? You seemed pretty eager to get started, yourself, when we were inside that house. I thought that you were going to jump right in and take over."

When the scared rookie protests that he or she is not ready yet, the sales manager smiles reassuringly, and says, "Don't worry, you'll have your chance, soon enough."

While the new rep is wondering what was meant by that last statement, he or she is relieved to see the manager knock on the next door, gain entrance, and set the stage for the next sales presentation. About halfway through, the boss suddenly glances at his or her watch and exclaims, "Oh, my gosh! Is it that late, already? I've got another appointment that can't wait. Hey kid, will you take this one over for me? Folks, I hope you won't mind, but I've gotta go." And the manager abruptly departs, leaving the rookie rep to sink or swim.

This is called "dumping," and many a newcomer has been dumped in a territory and dumped on afterward. Sometimes the prospect families feel so sorry for the victim that they give him or her their business. It's a bravado way of life in certain industries, and if you haven't been through this ordeal, you will never gain the respect of your peers and subordinates who have. It's a perverse form of maverick pride and honor.

Dumping in the 'Burbs

Another variation of the sink-or-swim school of outside field sales training is to drive a group of unsuspecting new recruits off into a remote suburb — or distant hinterlands — where there are no public transportation facilities available after a certain evening hour. Each rookie is dumped off in a separate area which is far apart from each other, with instructions to be at a particular place, such as a street corner at a specific time.

Since there are no other means of returning from the field for at least several hours, these aspiring salespeople have only two options:

1. Go to work — make the desired cold calls in the area, canvassing the neighborhood
2. Be arrested by the police for loitering

Talk about a tightly controlled training system! You can see why power bosses favor this method of field indoctrination. They view their sales force as merely a collection of warm bodies and arms and legs who are expendable. Unfortunately these attitudes and practices give professional selling and sales management a bad reputation.

Range Riding with Veteran Mavericks

When working with your more experienced salespeople, outside sales training takes on the form of coaching. It is the next step in the natural evolution of your continuous sales training program. It focuses on building leader/member relationships, strengthening selling skills, reinforcing knowledge, pointing out opportunities for improvement, and stimulating your staff to higher levels of productivity and accomplishment.

Coaching is a supportive activity in which you observe your veterans on customer sales calls and then provide guidance and constructive criticism. It can be a severe test of your teaching and sensitivity skills which will enable you to influence the behavior, selling styles, and attitudes of your mavericks. Coaching is certainly no easy assignment, as some sales managers lack confidence in their mentoring abilities, fear failure when demonstrating their own unorthodox selling methods—particularly in front of seasoned sales reps—and are often reluctant to criticize them through fear of disturbing fragile relationships.

Coaching Procedure

Before you saddle up, you should review the files of the reps that you are going to coach so that you are familiar with all significant aspects of their past and present performance. Problems in the territory will influence your itinerary planning as well as your coaching approach. Make a checklist of those items you want to cover with each individual salesperson. One intensive day of coaching at a time, stretched over a number of months, should be enough to do the job. Anything more amounts to overkill.

Approach your seasoned veterans as one professional to another. Treat them with dignity and respect. Confer on the game plan. They will do the selling, you the observing. Your role is not to sell but to develop salespeople who can. Before each account call, you should ask them a series of questions which will help them improve their ability to plan their account development:

1. *How much business have you done with this account to date? What is their potential?*
   Get them to think in terms of account potentials and profitable sales volume.

2. *Who are your main contacts here? Are they decision makers, decision influencers, or underlings?*
   Get them to sell in-depth and identify the buying centers of each customer.

3. *What customer problems are you solving with our product line or service package?*

Get them to understand that a product or service is a tool that solves a customer problem.

4. *Are there other areas where we can serve this client?*
Get them to see that they are selling solutions and not merely pushing product.

5. *How much do you know about each individual in this account's chain of command? What are their personal and professional needs?*
Get them to understand that people are buying relationships rather than products and services.

6. *What obstacles stand in the way of our complete development of this account, and what can you do about them?*
Get them to think it terms of individual account strategies and that they have home office support to draw upon.

7. *What is your game plan for this account? Where do you go from here?*
This is another strategy thought-provoker.

8. *Which products and/or services will you offer this prospect? Why? How will you present them?*
Get them to think through their product or service offerings and the sequence of their sales presentation.

9. *How much sales volume do you estimate will come from this customer and why?*
Get them to forecast sales on an individual account basis as realistically as possible.

10. *What is your call objective with this account?*
Get them to focus on objectives and desired results. There might be better places to spend their time.

Making the Joint Call

As previously stated, your rep runs this show and you observe his or her behavior. Watch how the rep handles receptionists, secretaries, and shop workers as well as his or her key account contacts. What does he or she do with spare time while waiting in the lobby for a prospect or faced with a broken appointment. Does the maverick make any cold calls, visit any tough customers, or merely call on "old friends" who will make him or her look good in your eyes? You should see a blend of accounts and selling situations.

Besides observing the rep's client interpersonal relationships and selling style, you evaluate his or her appearance, attire, speaking voice, and general deportment during these visits. Make mental notes of any specific areas which you would like to address at your critique session at the end of the day. Sometimes it might serve a useful purpose for you to handle a complete sales call so that your maverick can view you in action. This is another instance of leading by example. Never tell him or her to do anything that you can't do or have never done, or your credibility will go down the drain.

Concluding Your Field Training Sessions

After each joint sales call there is a great temptation — and a lot of rep pressure — to discuss what took place. Except for an obvious blunder, you want to limit these curbside critiques to one or two major aspects of the visit and defer the rest until the end of the day. At that time you will review the entire day's work in a more formalized and structured manner.

After the last account call of the day, you should sit down in private with your maverick and have a somewhat lengthy gab session regarding some general conclusions that you have reached about his or her current abilities and future selling capabilities. These conclusions are based upon specific observations which you made and discussed during your various curbside conferences. This is not the time to rehash every gory detail of those critiques or introduce any other negative aspects of the performance. Instead, focus on the salesperson's opportunities for improvement and outline the actions you expect him or her to take in order to overcome deficiencies and capitalize on opportunities for self-development.

Do not hesitate to candidly discuss whatever problems in the rep's delivery that you have discovered, but don't make them appear bigger than they really are. Keep your discussion positive and concentrate on one major point at a time. You can mention the ideas of other mavericks who have dealt successfully with some of the same problems. Compliment your reps on the way they handled a particular aspect of your joint calls. Even the most jaded veterans want to be appreciated and know how they're doing. Whenever you single out techniques that they used in an effective manner, you are strengthening and reinforcing the future use of those techniques. Your use of the psychological learning principles of repetition, reinforcement, and summation are especially effective in shaping field selling behavior and sharpening skills. This style of coaching is extremely effective because it is perceived as guidance rather than criticism.

Now that you are acquainted with the essentials of coaching and training, test your new-found expertise on the Sales Manager's Quiz which concludes this chapter. The correct answers can be found in Chap. 13, "The Sales Manager's Manual." Good luck.

Coaching Summary

Most experienced mavericks are receptive to feedback from a mentor figure who has observed them in action. Be it positive or negative, such feedback has a powerful impact on a professional salesperson's attitude, since nothing motivates better than the prospect of improving one's effectiveness and achieving greater selling success. Conscientious, consistent, and tactful curbside coaching and formal review sessions mean that at the end of the day you will have a better, more effective, and more highly motivated maverick than the one you started out with that morning.

Granted, it's harder for a new sales manager to succeed in this challenging area at first than for an incumbent sales team leader, but you've got to give it your best shot. Teach them everything that you know. Become the expert coach and teacher of your company. Invest in knowledge and personal growth. Send your reps published materials covering their individual areas of weaknesses as well as current books and tapes on selling techniques. Learn to replace yourself, lest your fear of experienced maverick competition become a barrier to your own growth within your firm. You've got what it takes for field leadership or you wouldn't have been promoted to the sales management position in the first place. If you believe in yourself and always strive to reach your full executive potential by helping others to reach theirs, you will become not only a successful coach, trainer, and teacher but also a truly effective sales manager.

The Silver Stirrup Award

The Silver Stirrup Award is given to new mavericks after their first coaching session in the field. It symbolizes the *support* that you gave them during their "breaking in" period. Now they're ready to convert all of that knowledge into sales volume. They'll earn their spurs when they make quota. The coveted Golden Spur Award goes to the top salesperson in the company for the year. Those mavericks who don't make quota are given the gate.

Chapter 9 Roundup

Riding shotgun in the field with your mavericks is the best known way of implementing inside-classroom training. New reps gain confidence and begin to write orders. Veterans become rejuvenated. With experienced salespeople, this management method evolves into individualized coaching and performance monitoring. Both sales management activities reinforce the learning process and are highly motivational because of the personal recognition and self-improvement factors. The Silver Stirrup Award is presented to new mavericks after their first outside training session. Another potential selling superstar has been born because of your fine teaching and coaching.

Sales Manager's Self-Quiz

This petite self-quiz will test your expertise on coaching and training skills. You will either agree or disagree with the statements that follow—there's no middle ground. Be decisive! The correct answers and their explanations can be found in "The Sales Manager's Manual," Chap. 13. Now, go for it!

1. You have made it abundantly clear to your mavericks that you will always be available to help close a sale if you are needed. Is this a good idea?

Yes _____ No _____

2. Do you insist that your reps not deviate from a standard closing technique?

Yes _____ No_____

3. Despite a good presentation, salesperson Smith cannot get the purchase order. With the prior approval of her manager, Smith offers the customer an exclusive deal, something for the customer's firm alone. Do you approve of Smith's closing tactic?

Yes _____ No _____

4. Do you know what kinds of closes your sales reps are using?

Yes _____ No _____

5. You have conducted a training session on closing techniques within the past year.

Yes _____ No _____

6. You like to have your credit manager or engineering specialist present when a major client is likely to buy.

Yes _____ No _____

7. Do you agree with this statement: "Sixty percent of the time, mavericks never actually ask for the order"?

Yes _____ No _____

8. Do you apply pressure on your credit department to speed up its decision making?

Yes _____ No _____

9. Whenever possible, salesperson Jones's builds his close around an offer to match the competition's bid. He says, "It's dramatic, and buyers find it hard to refuse the chance to save themselves some money." Do you approve of Jones's closing technique?

Yes _____ No_____

10. A good closing method is to ask the client outright—but at the right moment—"Well, how about it? May I have the factory ship you a carload?" Do you agree?

Yes _____ No _____

11. Your compensation program awards bonuses for *booked orders* rather than for orders shipped.

Yes _____ No _____

12. Your firm's visual aids (flip charts, read-off presentation, film scripts, etc.) each have several built-in opportunities to let your client say yes.

Yes _____ No _____

13. You pay your mavericks a higher incentive for closing sooner than later.

Yes _____ No _____

14. Do you accompany your sales team members to observe their closing techniques?

Yes _____ No _____

15. Do you allow your mavericks as much leeway as possible on prices and delivery?

Yes _____ No _____

16. Sales reps differ widely on what they consider to be a close. Do you agree?

Yes _____ No _____

17. A good rule is "Get the order and get the hell out of there." Do you agree?

Yes _____ No _____

18. "If the rep's not interested in money, I'm not interested in them." Do you concur?

Yes _____ No _____

19. You have read a book, magazine article, or taken a seminar on sales management within the past year.

Yes _____ No _____

20. Manipulator/facilitator personalities are the most effective sales managers.

Yes _____ No _____

10
Motivating Mavericks

Nothing great was ever achieved without enthusiasm.   RALPH WALDO EMERSON

Introduction to Motivation

Motivating mavericks is one of the most challenging tasks for a newly appointed sales manager. It's tough enough for veterans who know their sales team members more intimately. The truth is that you cannot motivate people to do anything, but you can create a working environment in which *they will want to motivate themselves.* The best that you can do is to hope that your words and actions—or lack of action—will not *demotivate* your salespeople. How you handle the following true-life story will reveal your capabilities as a motivator of mavericks.

Case Study
The Elevator Story—
A True-Life Experience

On the way to work one morning, a general insurance agent (local sales manager) entered a crowded elevator in her high-rise office building. Two affluent-looking executives squeezed into the elevator just before the doors closed. As the elevator slowly ascended, she overheard the following conversation:

> EXECUTIVE A: "Last night my attorney and I were reviewing my estate planning, and we discovered that I am grossly under insured. Do you know a good insurance agent?"

EXECUTIVE B: "It's odd that you should bring that subject up. My spouse and I had the very same discussion and reached the identical conclusion. We need more insurance too! Do you happen to know a good insurance provider? We've got to buy some additional coverage, but quick!"

Now put yourself in this general insurance sales manager's boots. There you are — squashed up against the back wall of the crowded elevator — and you overhear two hot prospects speaking. They desperately want to buy what you've got to sell. *What should you do?*

A word of caution: Before you act, make sure that you are thinking like a manager and not a doer (salesperson) and that you understand the motivational implications of your actions.

This savvy sales manager resisted the strong temptation to write up these two easy orders on the spot. Instead, she got off the elevator at the same floor as these two hot prospects, followed them to their respective offices, noted their locations, and then returned to her own office. There, she immediately called a sales meeting and reiterated most of her elevator experience. She carefully omitted the names or office locations of the prospects. Instead, she removed a $100 bill from her purse and waved it before her startled subordinates, saying, "Somewhere in *this* magnificent office building complex is at least one, and possibly *two* easy orders, just waiting to be written up. Here's a hundred dollar bonus for the first person to get either order!"

What do you think happened? What do you think was the motivational impact on her salespeople? Now look at what you decided to do. If you had opted for the personal satisfaction and commissions from writing up one or both of these orders, you've missed the management boat. You are still thinking and acting like a salesperson and not like a sales manager. In this instance, doing — writing up the order — was motivational for yourself but *demotivational for your sales staff.* Compare this short-term thinking with what actually happened.

The sales force literally went wild. While searching for those two "easy" orders, those insurance agents tore that office building apart! In fact, they set an all-time agency record for order production in a single day! This shrewd sales executive not only made more override commission money on these subordinates' sales than she could ever have made from writing up these "elevator sales" herself but also energized her sales team to reach new heights of accomplishment. Her motivational method was much preferable to the usual bland appeals for cold calling, and she was even willing to spice up her appeal with an extra couple of $100 bills, for good measure.

The ironic aftermath of this incredible record-sales day was the discovery that *both* prospects had been missed by her sales force! In their frantic anxiety, they somehow failed to catch up with the original prospects. I leave it to your imagination what she said to them on the following business day.

The Behavioral Components of Motivation

Motivation is behavior that is instigated by needs within an individual and directed toward goals that can satisfy those needs. A *need* is a lack of anything that is desired, required, or useful. Abraham H. Maslow, the father of humanist psychology, theorized that human wants form a hierarchy of importance, as shown in Fig. 10-1. As a need of a lower order is being satisfied, it becomes less and less important, and a need of the next highest order becomes more and more important. Maslow applied to human wants what might be called a marginal utility of needs with economic want at the bottom of the hierarchy and self-fulfillment

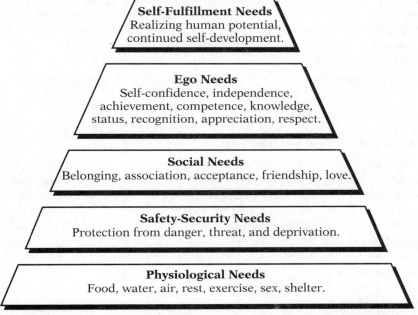

Figure 10-1. Maslow's Hierarchy of Human Needs. (*Source: Abraham H. Maslow,* Motivation and Personality, *Second Edition, Harper & Row, New York, 1970. Reprinted with permission of HarperCollins Publishers.*)

at the top. Perhaps that's why money, in itself, may not be a prime motivator, but real, or perceived, earnings differentials definitely motivate mavericks. A glance at the free agents' market in professional sports indicates that this is the underlying factor in most superstar negotiations. Why should it be any different in professional selling? You're still dealing with human beings and their needs.

Maslow, Herzberg, and McGregor Can Help You

This triumvirate of motivational mavericks developed different psychological theories of motivation which can help you create a stimulating working environment in your own sales organization. An essential starting point is to understand the needs that drive your individual mavericks. Each salesperson has a personal style and agenda. Your task is to satisfy his or her psychological needs within an organizational context. No easy job!

From Maslow's hierarchy of needs theory, we can learn that money's effectiveness as a motivator declines as a sales rep ascends the needs hierarchy. Money is very important to satisfy the lower-level needs, such as physiological needs and safety-security needs. To satisfy the higher-level wants, such as self-esteem and self-actualization, however, various kinds of recognition awards or promotions to higher status positions or more desirable assignments will be more effective.

Maslow and *Your* Mavericks

If you know the needs that drive your mavericks, you can shape their behaviors. Although not perfect matches, there are some strong linkages between the personality categories I've introduced throughout and the Maslow model. Let's begin at the bottom of Maslow's Hierarchy of Human Needs—physiological and safety-security needs. That's the natural habitat of the avoider/abdicator, who's always afraid of being fired. These are your below-average order producers whose prime motivation is *survival* on the job.

Moving upward in this ranked order of human wants, we find the affiliator/pleaser, who is motivated by social needs. The craving for friendship and acceptance can be seen in all of his or her endeavors. The power boss/commander dominates the next upward rung—ego needs. Everything that he or she does makes a powerful statement of self-importance. Although achiever/technicians have ego gratification needs, their main motivation comes from self-fulfillment and achievement—the work itself, as long as it is challenging.

Where does the manipulator/facilitator fit into the motivational picture? All over, at every need level. They could be motivated to overcome fear of failure, to gain social acceptance, or to reach their full potential as human beings. They are relatively ego-detached but take private pride in their grand accomplishments. In other words, manipulators are so flexible and elusive that they are hard to pin down into one specific need level at any particular time so that it seems to be more difficult to motivate them than the other four personality types. Being overly ambitious, they are best placed at the self-actualization need level. Most likely these mavericks are self-motivated and do not require any outside stimuli.

Now that you've identified the needs that drive your reps, you can develop individual-specific strategies for managing each of them. Being aware of the psychological implications of Herzberg's Motivation-Hygiene Theory and McGregor's Theory X and Theory Y (both discussed below) will add another important dimension to your personnel management activities. You want to create a stimulating win-win environment whereby both the organization and your individual salespeople benefit.

Herzberg's Motivation-Hygiene Theory

The Motivation-Hygiene Theory* of Frederick Herzberg recognizes only two levels of needs: hygiene needs (lower level) and motivational needs (higher level). Herzberg's motivational needs are comparable to Maslow's higher-level needs of esteem and status as well as self-actualization. The hygiene, or maintenance, needs are more basic. Simply stated, the maintenance factors attracted your mavericks to your company, but they will not cause them to set any order-production records. Motivational factors, if judiciously applied, will. See Fig. 10-2 for a comparison of the Maslow and Herzberg theories, then try to place individual members of your sales team in the appropriate slots. The integration of these overlapping models will enable you to motivate each of your mavericks according to his or her specific need structure.

---

*Material adapted from Frederick Herzberg, *Work and the Nature of Man*, Thomas Y. Crowell Co., New York, 1966.

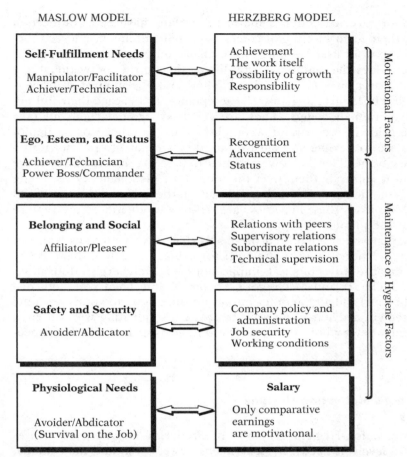

MASLOW MODEL   HERZBERG MODEL

Figure 10-2. Integration of the personality profiles with the Maslow and Herzberg theories.   Both the Maslow and Herzberg theories emphasize the same set of human relationships. Maslow focuses on the needs of the psychological person on the job, or anywhere else. Herzberg centers on that same individual in the working environment. Understanding the needs which drive each of your maverick personality types will enable you to select the appropriate appeals to galvanize them to action. (*Source: Frederick Herzberg,* Work and the Nature of Man, *Thomas Y. Crowell Co., New York, 1966.*)

McGregor's Theory X and Theory Y

Effective motivation is the product of the psychological needs of your individual salespeople and the motivational climate of your sales organization. Douglas M. McGregor, a professor at the Massachusetts Institute of Technology's Sloan School of Management, advocated that the job environment of an individual is *the most important variable affecting his or her development and performance.* Relationships develop from the assumptions which people bring to a job situation. Because authority figures have more influence than their subordinates, their assumptions are more controlling. Sales managers get back the result of what they input or assume. Conflict results from Theory X; cooperation is the fruit of Theory Y. You always reap what you sow. Thus, your style of leadership and expectations have a profound effect on the performance and morale of your sales organization. Figure 10-3 presents the gist of McGregor's Theory X and Theory Y.

Halo and Horns Effects

Here are some examples of how your attitude and assumptions about subordinates can cause you to make some choice blunders during the hiring and indoctrination stages. In the first instance, you have just hired a young dude who has recently graduated from your old alma mater. He also reminds you of yourself when you were about the same age. You are absolutely certain that he is going to be a real winner — just like you.

Strangely enough, he fails miserably on the first assignment that you give him. Don't worry, you tell your fellow managers. Be patient and give the kid a break. He'll be all right, you'll see. When he flubs up on the second task, you claim that he didn't have enough staff support to do the job right. On the third endeavor, the results are also quite poor, but you will not recognize or accept the fact that this young maverick is an obvious loser.

This is the "halo effect." You have placed an imaginary halo around his head, and he can do no evil as far as you are concerned. He is also a projection of your own personality needs and a reflection of your hiring and training expertise — or lack of it!

Now consider the second scenario: you are compelled to hire this brash young dudette because of your firm's affirmative action program. In your sexist heart of hearts, you believe that women do not belong in sales, but you are stuck with her. Although she performs brilliantly on her first assignment, you chalk it off to "beginner's luck." When she succeeds superbly on her second task, you demur, claiming that a blind gorilla with sunglasses could have done as well. When she continues to achieve, you refuse to recognize her superior abilities because you have affixed a big set of horns to her head. While the loser with the "halo" can do no wrong, this fine winner can never do anything right for you. This is the "horns effect."

Consider the motivational and demotivational implications of playing favorites within your sales organization and how your daily behavior sends out strong signals to everyone. In fact, your expectations may send such strong signals to your reps that they unconsciously make your dreams (or nightmares) come true.

Theory X: **The Traditional View of Direction and Control**

1. The average human being has an inherent dislike of work and will avoid it if he or she can.
2. Because of this human characteristic of dislike of work, most people must be coerced, controlled, directed, and threatened with punishment to get them to put forth adequate effort toward the achievement of organizational objectives.
3. The average human being prefers to be directed, wishes to avoid responsibility, has relatively little ambition, and wants security above all.

Theory Y: **The Integration of Individual and Organizational Goals**

1. The expenditure of physical and mental effort in work is as natural as in play or rest.
2. External control and the threat of punishment are not the only means for bringing about effort toward organizational objectives. People will exercise self-direction and self-control in the service of objectives to which they are committed.
3. Commitment to objectives is a function of the rewards associated with their achievement.
4. The average human being learns, under proper conditions, not only to accept but to seek responsibility.
5. The capacity to exercise a relatively high degree of imagination, ingenuity, and creativity in the solution of organizational problems is widely, not narrowly, distributed in the population.
6. Under the conditions of modern industrial life, the intellectual potentialities of the average human being are only partially utilized.

Figure 10-3. McGregor's Theory X and Theory Y. (*Source: Douglas McGregor*, The Human Side of Enterprise, *McGraw-Hill Book Company, New York, 1960, pp. 33–34 and 47–48.*)

Self-Fulfilling Prophesies

Although managers' expectations can sometimes blind them to the true worth of their reps (as in the halo and horns effects), many times it is the expectations of sales managers that *determine* the achievement of the individual, as well as that of the group. Numerous studies have been made that document Herzberg's "Pygmalion effect" in leader/member relationships. Most notable was the

"Sweeney's Miracle" in which the high expectations of Professor George Sweeney transformed a young janitor into a computer whiz. The following is another bizarre situation, which occurred during an annual sales meeting.

Case Study

The Case of the Mysterious Hotel Rooms

A company president was engaged to address the sales force at their annual sales meeting in Florida. He was called a "three-by-five" executive, not because of his height and weight but because of his propensity to rely on three-by-five cards for everything that he did. Since the salespeople were divided into groups based on their sales quota performance and assembled in three different meeting rooms, the prexy was given the following three-by-five-card information: Parlor A contained the winners. These reps had made their sales quota this year and had usually reached or exceeded it in previous years. Parlor B held the also-rans. These hard-working salespeople almost made quota but just missed it. Apparently they all had been in this position for years. Guess who was in Parlor C? These were the outright losers—they weren't even close and hadn't been for years. That was the selling scenario for the president's speech. Based on this three-by-five-card input, he proceeded to address the occupants of each hotel meeting room as follows:

> PARLOR A: You guys and gals are the greatest! I knew that you could do it. We are all proud of you. We know that you will do it again next year. Rah! Rah! Rah! etc.

Result: Next year every member of Parlor A made quota or exceeded it. The winners continued to win big.

> PARLOR B: Well, folks, almost only counts in horseshoes. We know how hard you tried, even though you didn't make quota. Just keep on trying, and one day you might make it, perhaps next year. In the meantime, lots of luck.

Result: Next year they all stumbled out into the field and once again, just barely missed making quota.

> PARLOR C: Well, guys and gals, I guess you all know why you're gathered here in this hotel room. But don't worry, no one's going to get fired. Not yet, anyhow. It might not happen until next year, unless you shape up first. In the meantime, hang in there, baby!

Result: Next year they all staggered back into their respective territories and failed again miserably.

Since this sales meeting and its aftermath were considered to be reasonably successful, the company president was invited back to give the same kind of motivational speech to the sales mavericks the following year. The time and location were the same, but the hotel had a new banquet manager who inadvertently switched the meeting rooms around. He put the losers in Parlor A, the winners in Parlor B, and the also-rans in Parlor C. Unfortunately the president was not informed of the mysterious hotel room switch, so he proceeded to his usual three-by-five-card speeches. The chief executive talked to the occupants of each room in the same inspirational manner as in the previous year. What do you think happened?

> PARLOR A: You guys and gals are terrific! We at the home office knew that you could do it, etc.

Result: Since he was addressing the loser group, the president was greeted with incredulous stares and blank looks. Nobody in their lives had ever spoken to them in such positive or encouraging terms. Nevertheless, after awhile they all got caught up in the enthusiasm of the moment and started to get excited about their jobs. The next year, for the first time in their lives, some of these losers actually made quota. Despite their past unbroken record of failure, they became winners.

> PARLOR B: [Instead of the winner's-circle speech which they were accustomed to hearing at these annual sales meetings, these winners now heard nonsensical talk about horseshoes, also-rans, and "trying" to succeed.]

Result: They could hardly believe their ears. Company president or not, *nobody* had ever talked to them in that disparaging manner before. For the first time in their championship lives, some of these high achievers actually failed to make their sales quotas for the next fiscal year. Some of these winners had suddenly regressed to also-rans.

> PARLOR C: [Instead of the "horseshoe" talk and "trying hard," the also-rans now heard consoling comments about "hanging in there" and "collective kicks in the pants" if they didn't improve.]

Result: Next year they became instantaneous losers. Not even one of these also-rans lived up to their group name. Where they all had previously just missed reaching quota in past years, now they weren't even close! They had, in fact, become losers. Why did this strange phenomenon occur?

The Expectations of the Leader
Become the Achievement of the Group

This story* illustrates Frederick Herzberg's self-fulfilling prophecy theory, or the Pygmalion effect, in management. Because the expectations

---

*Material adapted from Frederick Herzberg, *Work and the Nature of Man*, Thomas Y. Crowell Co., New York, 1966.

of the leader become, in fact, the achievement of the group, your attitude toward your mavericks and your management assumptions will be reflected in their job performance. If you believe that they can reach their selling potential, while communicating this faith in their abilities, they will succeed admirably. They will even move mountains for you. On the other hand, if you have strong doubts or reservations about their capabilities, this will be reflected in lackluster performance.

You can encourage your mavericks to excel by establishing a positive and supportive working climate, giving prompt feedback, and reinforcing desired behaviors. Make it known that you want to help them achieve their goals and that you are available for counsel and advice. Your attitude and behavior can motivate your reps and contribute directly to their selling successes and failures. Although true motivation comes from within, there are four basic methods of motivating mavericks.

Main Types of Motivation

The four main methods of motivation vary from short-term to long-term effectiveness. Many times their use is directly related to the personality needs of the sales manager.

Fear Motivation

Benito Mussolini, the Italian dictator during World War II, said, "To make a people great it is necessary to send them to battle, even if you have to kick them in the pants." Like the ill-fated *Il Duce,* some power boss/commander sales managers still believe that there are only 19 inches between a pat on the back and a kick on the rear. With today's new breed of reps, a slap on the back and a kick in the pants won't work anymore, but this method is still being used in some quarters.

Fear motivation causes a person to act or refrain from acting through fear of the consequences. This technique is considered negative because penalties and punishments are emphasized. Fear motivation is the application of Theory X to sales management. This traditional view of employee direction and control states that the typical maverick salesperson is lazy, dislikes work, and will avoid it if possible. Power bosses and achievers think that their salespeople are nothing more than a bunch of avoiders when it comes to getting the sales job done.

According to this view, because of this inherent dislike of work, most mavericks must be coerced, controlled, driven, and threatened with all kinds of punishments to get them to put forth adequate effort toward the attainment of departmental objectives. Thus, in the opinion of these managers, the average rep prefers to be directed, wishes to avoid responsibility, has relatively little ambition, and desires security above all.

Having this negative attitude toward subordinates, it is easy to understand why fear motivation is the power boss's main method of relating to his or her salespeople. A typical motivational appeal like this is frequently heard: "One mistake and you're fired!" A more enlightened approach is "If you do a good job this week, you get to keep it. However, if you mess things up and lose that account, then you've got two weeks and jolly good luck!"

Some timorous souls — particularly avoider/abdicators, affiliator/pleasers, and a few achiever/technicians — are strongly influenced by the fear of the loss of commissions, personal dignity, self-esteem, or their jobs. An affiliator rep will do anything to keep the peace if the boss is angry with him, her, or the entire sales team. They are the peace makers and compromisers in the group and want everybody to be happy all the time. Withholding recognition or praise, as well as making threats, can be highly motivational to them in a negative sort of way. (Try not saying "Good morning" to one of your affiliators and watch what happens: Before you can hang up your hat, that person will be in your office wondering what's wrong, and why you're angry with him or her!)

Other sales team members may also be motivated by the fear of losing their jobs, being transferred to less desirable territories, or suffering a cut in pay. When used too frequently or with too much severity, fear motivation can result in recipient withdrawal. Some salespeople will tend to flee or otherwise avoid this kind of destructive stimulation if they can rather than change their behavior as desired by the stimulator. That might explain why you might catch some of your mavericks in a movie theater taking in a weekday matinee performance instead of being out in the field facing the music, or you — whichever they feel is the lesser of the two evils. Thus, if they cannot run away or hide from an ego-threatening situation, some reps will become calloused, hostile, or just plain phlegmatic.

A maverick confronted with the loss of physical comfort, security, or a feeling of personal acceptance will soon find other means of satisfying those basic needs, and then the impact of the threat evaporates into thin air. As you see, fear motivation is essentially short-term in effectiveness. Even worse, it tends to be negative and totally destructive in terms of leader/member relationships and team building. Fear motivation often results in poor or grudging performance, and rarely, if ever, are mavericks spurred onward and upward to greater productivity or superior achievements just to keep the boss off their backs. A form of group passive resistance soon sets in and blunts all forward progress.

Nevertheless, in spite of its considerable drawbacks, fear motivation

and autocratic leadership do have legitimate places in sales management when used sparingly and selectively. Authoritarianism is still practiced by the majority of corporations, and fear motivation is a prevalent
operating mode. Let's be honest with ourselves and our mavericks—
sometimes a little butt-kicking goes a long way! Just don't do it too often. That's part of the Code of the Old West, where an occasional horse-
whipping comes with the territory.

Incentive Motivation

Incentive motivation consists of the promise of a reward of some kind
for the attainment of a goal or an objective. It is at the opposite end of
the motivational spectrum from fear motivation because rewards are
promised and positives are emphasized. This method is very popular
with affiliator/pleaser sales managers because they like to please their
reps, believing that everyone is stimulated by incentives to a certain degree, some more than others. People work to earn money to buy the
necessities of life and the luxuries they desire. Money is an incentive
only if we want what it will buy. Added or extra compensation is only an
inducement if your reps want what that extra compensation will buy
badly enough to do the extra work to earn it.

If your mavericks' needs for self-confidence and attention are greater than their
needs for the things that money can buy, then praise and recognition will have
an equal or greater incentive value than money, until self-confidence is re-
stored. Since inducements to work are based upon needs, then following the
marginal utility aspects of Maslow's theory, when each need has been satisfied,
this incentive no longer has the power to motivate behavior. Once the money
need is satisfied, a salesperson will cease putting forth the extra effort to get it.
The impact of monetary incentives as an enticement for your reps to do extra
work will be short-lived and is subject to the law of diminishing returns.

Furthermore, when used too frequently, money incentives tend to be
taken for granted as part of what your reps expect as base pay or normal treatment for merely acceptable, but not exceptional, work. Money
of itself, as a motivator will rarely cause a sustained increase in order
productivity. Therefore, you should concentrate your efforts on the
recognition aspects of incentive motivation.

Although incentive motivation should be built into sales force compensation plans and performance quota systems, it may also be used effectively in sales contests and other award programs where outstanding
achievement is recognized. The more recognition that you can give
your mavericks, the better. Do it at every opportunity and in a variety of
creative ways. Remember what Henry David Thoreau said: "This world
is but canvas to our imaginations."

Some suggestions can be found in Chap. 13, "The Sales Manager's

Manual." Hopefully, you will add some of your own ideas and experiences to this important area of sales management. Keep in mind, however, that although incentive motivation is probably the most popular method of stimulating employees, it tends to be short-term in effectiveness.

Attitude Motivation

Attitude motivation is the process of helping your mavericks modify their attitudes and strengthen their self-images so that they can become authentic human beings and effective salespeople. It is based upon the valid assumption that people naturally want to do a good job and are willing to change. This is the view of Douglas McGregor's Theory Y Management, where there is an integration of individual and organizational goals.

Unlike the Theory X, or autocratic leadership, view of their subordinates' attitudes toward their jobs, Theory Y sales managers believe that the expenditure of physical and mental effort in work is as natural as play or rest and that external control and the threat of punishment are not the only means for bringing about successful effort toward the attainment of organizational objectives.

Manipulator/facilitator and affiliator/pleaser sales managers believe that their mavericks will exercise self-direction and self-control in the service of goals to which they are committed. They feel that commitment to objectives is a function of the rewards associated with their achievement. The average salesperson learns—under proper conditions—not only to accept but to seek responsibility; he or she has the capacity to exercise a relatively high degree of imagination, ingenuity, and creativity in the solution of territorial problems.

The motivational needs of your mavericks are directly related to their self-image and attitudes toward their jobs, their sales manager—you!—and their company. Attitudes, or habits of thought, are at the very heart of every salesperson's effectiveness and future growth potential. Your attitude toward your mavericks and the motivational climate of your organization has a great deal to do with their perception of the available opportunities. Motivational climate is a function of your firm's goals and its organizational attitude—policies, procedures, new product development, market expansion, financial stability, etc.

Your role in this process is to provide growth opportunities, encourage your salespeople to accept more responsibility, and maintain the kind of supportive work environment that fosters attitude change. Help them identify personal goals which can be achieved by their working toward company objectives. Therefore, you should encourage your mavericks to set goals for both their personal and professional lives. Get them to reach out for targets which they might think beyond them, stretch them toward superior success and escalating accomplishments.

If you can inspire your salespeople to proceed to bigger and better — and even tougher challenges as part of a coordinated sales team effort — they will all take pride and satisfaction in playing a winning hand. In this kind of exciting work environment, each player will realize his or her own contribution to the team's success and know that he or she is needed and appreciated. When you develop this kind of atmosphere, you don't have to rely on the carrot-or-stick stimulations of incentive and fear motivation.

Your task is to unlock whatever inhibitions or fetters of fear that prevent your mavericks from reaching their full potential as human beings and as professional salespeople. Because attitude change necessarily precedes behavioral change, you should focus on attitude motivation for best long-range results. If you can get your reps to accomplish more than they, themselves, ever thought possible, then their self-confidence will grow and their attitude toward you, their job, and their company will change for the better. Once their attitudes are modified, positive behavioral change is merely a matter of time...and more motivational input. The end result will be increased job commitment, higher morale, and reduced employee turnover. That's how to retain your mavericks.

Example Motivation

Example motivation means setting a positive example by your own daily conduct as coach, counselor, and sales team leader. It also consists of establishing high, challenging goals for your organization and assisting your sales force to reach or exceed them by following your earnest example. Successful sales managers earn the respect of their mavericks by their personal behavior. You can set the right example by emphasizing the following professional management attributes:

- Positive mental attitude
- Personal integrity and character
- Appropriate appearance
- Resourcefulness and flexibility
- Continual self-improvement in selling and training skills

Do not become an "inside administrator." Salespeople do not need the example of a fat-cat executive; they need the example of a successful salesperson and leader. A training lecture may be worth a thousand words, but an order written before a new rep in the field is worth a thousand lectures. Don't just tell 'em, *show* them how to do it! Be a player-coach. Teach them everything that you know about selling and provide opportunities for continuous growth and development. (This is a managing function because you are building sales skills by demonstrating how it's done.)

Set a good example; your team members will take their cues from you. If your work habits are good, theirs will be too. If your advice and counsel are expert, they will accomplish what you expect of them. Never accept less than maximum effort or reward mavericks for doing less than what you demand of them. Otherwise they will doubt your sincerity when rewarding appropriate acts and, even worse, expect perks for performing low-priority duties.

Motivational Summary

The four main methods of motivating mavericks include fear, incentive, attitude, and example motivation. The first two techniques are effective in short-term situations, whereas the latter pair cause long-term behavioral change. Each method has its advantages and disadvantages, but a selective use of each will produce desired results. Ultimately, your own personality needs will determine which motivational method you will favor and how effectively you will use it.

Fear motivation is an application of Theory X, and attitude motivation is directly related to Theory Y philosophy. To a certain extent, incentive motivational methods are derived from Theory Y thinking, but in the hands of affiliator/pleaser or avoider/abdicator sales managers, there is a tendency to "give the store away." Example motivation is effectively utilized by manipulator/facilitator, achiever/technician, and enlightened power boss sales managers. In practice, it is probably the most difficult method to consistently implement because you have so many "balls in the air" at one time and therefore your own character, attitudes, and behavior are constantly being tested by the daily pressures of your sales management job. Nevertheless, it is the most important of the four techniques.

Chapter 10 Roundup

This chapter introduced behavioral science concepts as a basis for motivating your mavericks. Maslow's Hierarchy of Human Needs, Herzberg's Motivation-Hygiene Theory, and McGregor's Theory X and Theory Y were presented as guidelines to the four main motivational methods you can use to stimulate your mavericks to exceptional performance. As in everything else you do in sales management, *your attitude* and feelings of self-confidence determine which techniques you will use and their effectiveness. Remember, you can lead a horse to water, but you can't make it drink. You've got to create a thirst for self-improvement.

11

Managing Mavericks

*The great thing in this world is not so much
where we stand, as in what direction we are
moving.* OLIVER WENDELL HOLMES, SR.

Introduction to Managing

Perhaps the most severe test of a new sales manager's executive capacity
is the management of his or her mavericks. Independent and somewhat
rebellious by nature, they can cause all kinds of organizational problems
in building cooperative team efforts. These diamonds-in-the-rough riders resent "cowtowing" to authority figures and frequently make the
managerial pot boil. Controlling maverick behavior, avoiding
demotivational traps, and developing new salespeople are the main issues addressed in this chapter.

The Case of the
Pillow-Talking Reps

A newly appointed sales manager was excited and gratified to receive a
number of long-distance congratulatory telephone calls from his salespeople. They all said that they were with important customers and
"couldn't talk," and they abruptly hung up. Soon after this ego-stroking
stopped, and the feelings of euphoria wore off, the novice executive
suddenly realized that one of these reps was with a notorious "problem"

account, so he called that salesperson back at the account's office. To his surprise, the client informed him that not only was that salesperson not there but he had not seen the scoundrel for at least six months!

Several phone calls later, the sales manager learned that this "star" salesperson was really at home in bed. It turned out that the rep just wanted to know where the new boss was and then give him some excuse or distraction, so that he would not "bug" him.

The disillusioned sales executive then proceeded to call back all of the other well-wishing mavericks to see if they were actually where they said they were. To his dismay, he soon discovered that none of them were where they said they were, and that the sandbag-the-boss game was in full swing. Most of these hustlers were at their homes making bedside calls.

After this mortifying "pillow-talk" experience, an older and wiser new sales manager now makes it a regular daily habit to do one of two things: He either calls all of his reps each morning at home — to make sure that they are indeed out of bed and off to work — or has these ambitious "self-starters" call in to his office from their first scheduled appointment each day. Otherwise, he is never quite sure that his sales force is even working!

A sad but true story from the annals of the Old West. Do you share the same concerns? Is control a problem, or is it a lack of motivation? Perhaps you inherited a bunch of deadbeats from your predecessor, or maybe they became demotivated by his or her policy and role behavior.

Demotivation can take a number of subtle forms besides the obvious lack of enthusiasm, employee turnover, and failure to achieve sales quota. How many times have you heard stories about the big order that's coming or claims that "the orders are right here on my desk," or "in my desk drawer," or the most famous myth of them all — "the order is in the mail" — but somehow they never seem to arrive? If these horror stories sound too familiar, then perhaps you should take a closer look at human nature and the demotivational traps that most newly appointed sales managers seem to fall into.

Demotivational Traps

As previously stated, the real problem in most sales organizations is not how to motivate salespeople but how to avoid demotivating them. Henry David Thoreau once observed, "If a man does not keep pace with his companions, perhaps he hears a different drummer." Most human beings, and particularly salespeople, are moved to action to fill a wide variety of personal and business needs. Although a satisfied need is not a motivator of behavior, an unsatisfied one is a demotivator.

A key element of motivation is the quality of leadership provided by the sales manager. If you are not perceived by your mavericks as competent, consistent, or fair, demotivation will surely occur. Be decisive; vacillation and procrastination confuse and discourage reps, peers, and superiors while playing into the hands of competitors. Inconsistencies in company policies, practices, and executive behavior can nullify even the most enlightened motivational strategies.

When positive reinforcement from sales managers is lacking, demotivation fills the gap. For example, security-motivated mavericks will be "turned on" by completely different factors in their job assignments than will recognition-motivated mavericks. Your task is to determine what are the appropriate motivators for each individual member of your sales team and to structure each person's work environment in a way that will enhance his or her potential for productive and self-rewarding activity.

The experience of your staff must be structured to allow them to broaden and deepen themselves so they can develop the character and skills needed for future sales management roles. Mavericks are best prepared to become sales executives when challenged at successively higher levels of responsibility. Without suitable stretching, their true potential is never fully realized. Becoming keenly sensitive to the values and psychological needs of others will enable you to avoid many of the demotivational traps described in this chapter.

Demotivators for Security-Motivated Mavericks

Security-motivated mavericks, such as the avoider/abdicator and affiliator/pleaser salespeople feel threatened by at least five different demotivational actions of their sales managers.

1. *Favoritism.*   Whether real or not, it is their perception of the threat to their security that counts.

2. *Arbitrary deprivation.*   The taking away of some aspect of their jobs, without giving them an adequate explanation demotivates these mavericks. This includes changes of territory, disallowance of some usual expense account item, taking away certain accounts, or changing their duties and responsibilities.

3. *Inattention or management by exception.*   This includes intentionally

ignoring them, or lack of attention unless a mistake is made, and then lots of negative comments. Inattention alone undermines security because security depends on recognition and reassurance. There is not enough "stroking" to assuage their feelings of insecurity.

4. *Criticism poorly given.*   Criticism of the reps, themselves, instead of the incident itself as a separate entity that you both can deal with at arm's length, constitutes a threat to the security-motivated maverick. Always criticize the *act* and not the person. Then you and your subordinate can communicate objectively rather than emotionally.

5. *Caste system and status symbols.*   All of the safe signs and indicators of belonging — especially to the in group — threaten those who are not members of that coveted group. A change in office location or a shrinkage of office space will also threaten security.

Demotivators for Recognition-Motivated Mavericks

Recognition-motivated mavericks, such as achiever/technician, power boss/commander, and affiliator/pleaser reps, are subject to an entirely different set of potential demotivators. Because they respond best to the challenges of some risk taking, the heady feeling of success and the accolades of their sales manager and clientele are very important to them. Working in a recognition vacuum, however, has the predictable opposite effect. Here are a few of the more devastating demotivators for this type of individual.

1. *Acceptance of second-rate work.*   Toleration of incompetence by you, or themselves, tends to depress the high level of productivity which, in turn, generates the needed recognition. That is why lowering your standards out of a misguided attempt to affiliate with your sales team members usually backfires with damaging long-term repercussions.

2. *Intolerance of mistakes.*   This is the other foolish extreme. To succeed, a certain amount of risk taking is necessary. In the process of either pursuing or closing a new account, opening up a new territory, etc., sometimes blunders are made and failures occur. If you or your reps cannot tolerate mistakes, the spur to action is stifled. If you, yourself, cannot face up to your *own* mistakes — or even worse, blame them on someone else — then you will discourage the entrepreneurial spirit of adventure and accomplishment in your department. Everyone must pay their dues, and flub-ups are part of the price of

success. Show me someone who has never failed, and I'll show you a liar. That's part of the folklore of the Old West.

3. *Poor feedback, either good or bad.* Recognition is the internal fuel which urges the recognition-motivated maverick to action. Applause and adulation are their oxygen. Poor feedback, either in frequency or quality, reduces their initiative. The most important element in establishing and maintaining a stimulating atmosphere is your insistence on free, open, and honest communications up and down the ranks. Prompt feedback and the utmost candor are at the very heart of good sales management. Nothing can destroy morale quicker than a prolonged communications breakdown. It is particularly demoralizing to a recognition-motivated maverick.

4. *Inflexible organization with rigid policies and procedures.* These factors inhibit the potential for personal contribution and subsequent recognition. Subordination of individual accomplishments to company procedures leaves no room for outstanding achievement and the hoped-for recognition which would result. This severe management attitude is reflected in the following comments:

"We've never done *that* before!"
"Oh, we tried that once before, and it didn't work."
"*No!* That's against company policy. You ought to know that. Check the sales manual."

That's why your pragmatic interpretation of your firm's policies and procedures has such a tremendous impact on sales force performance. Don't always go by the book, or the letter of the law, go by its spirit. Avoider/abdicator sales managers are guilty of extreme rigidity in these matters, so be flexible. Bend the rules, or you risk breaking the rep.

5. *Fear of conflict or fear of competition.* When they are made to feel unfairly in competition with other sales team members—such as the veteran sales rep Harvey Blue from our case in Chap. 4—recognition-motivated reps adopt a facade of complacency or indifference. They feel, and rightly so, "If I can't hope to win, why even try?" In the case in Chap. 4, an incentive motivational device—a sales contest—had become a demotivator for the rest of the sales force.

Yet, even when they cannot hope to compete successfully with their colleagues, these mavericks continue to need recognition. The question now becomes How do you relieve them of this frustration and get them back on track? How do you undo the damage that you have caused? Competition with *themselves* is the answer. If you have inherited an unfairly balanced competition within your organization, you can change it by having your mavericks compete with their own previous year's record instead of with each other. This will not be feasible, of course, if your industry is currently in a recession. (Whoever said that sales management was easy?)

Be flexible and sensitive to the diverse individual needs and temperaments of your salespeople. Your challenging task is to identify each of your mavericks' "different drummers" and then tune into their different paces. Bring them up to your speed, but be careful that you do not demotivate them in the process.

Demotivational Summary

The motivational atmosphere of your organization has a direct bearing on how your reps perceive opportunities available to fill their personal needs and attain professional goals. Factors which have a positive impact on performance are sound operating policies that are consistently and fairly administered; favorable working conditions; equitable compensation plans; good working relationships with fellow sales team members, supervisors, and subordinates; status; security; and personal job satisfaction.

As far as your mavericks are concerned, the motivational climate of your organization has a distinct personality. It's a culture within a culture. Your leadership behavior helps shape that cultural personality. If you are going to be any good at motivation, you must learn how to interpret the direction and beliefs of your organizational environment in terms that will be credible and stimulating to your salespeople. And if you can do that, you will avoid most of the demotivational traps which ensnarl most new sales managers.

Rookie Manager Mistakes

Perhaps the most common mistake that new sales managers make is to "come down hard" on reps who resist their directives. Power boss and achiever executives view resistance as a challenge to their authority and tend to overreact. Avoiders are also guilty of this feeling. These misguided managers are initially pleased when an uncooperative maverick resigns, even when that rep's sales performance is above average.

Instead of recognizing that they need to learn how to manage these difficult salespeople in ways that will produce desired results, they see their jobs as enforcing discipline and requiring their mavericks to "walk the straight and narrow" and "knuckle under" their rigid leadership. Their mistakes become painfully evident in hindsight when they review the loss of profitable sales volume previously generated by these uncooperative reps who have been forced to resign. They may eventually learn that it's a sales manager's job to balance innovation and creativity with conformity. Sometimes it's old so soon, and smart so late!

Your leadership should inspire the degree of followership that is best for your kind of organization. You must orchestrate a win-win atmosphere in which every salesperson and each situation is handled according to need. Even the most saddle-sore range rider will respond favorably to the positive direction which you, the team leader, set.

It's the maverick's nature to handle the assigned territory in his or her own way; mavericks won't tolerate much interference from you or from the home office. Be sure that you don't overmanage this breed of salesperson, because you can stifle creativity and inhibit selling talent. Since the ultimate consideration is performance, you need to understand what motivates the maverick psychology and give mavericks territorial assignments which are appropriate to their unique personalities.

In the final analysis, you alone must determine if your organization is paying too high a price for the maverick's unorthodox behavior. You can tolerate their hell-raising tactics providing, of course, that they aren't detrimental to your customers, your company, or other salespeople. The material which follows will be helpful in establishing optimum sales team leader/member relationships and managing each of the five personality types.

Establishing Winning Leader/Member Relationships

Nothing tests a new sales manager's leadership ability more than taking over a veteran sales organization. Most people dislike change—even if it offers an improvement over the status quo. Some mavericks will exploit it for their own purposes and thereby disturb group cohesiveness. One of the keys to group acceptance and organizational control is the establishment of winning leader/member relationships.

Leader/member relationships are determined by the degree to which the sales team members support their sales manager and the potential for conflict or harmony within the ranks. By far, *the single most important element in situational control is the amount of loyalty and cooperation that you, the team leader, get from your subordinates.* If you can depend on them, you don't have to depend upon your position power or task structure to get compliance—your staff already accepts your directives. Furthermore, if your recommendations to *your* boss are accepted and approved, your reps will have even more confidence in your leadership.

The key issue is simply *How well do you and your mavericks get along?* Be sensitive to the ever-changing patterns of your salespeople's relationships with you and with each other. For this reason, you should make it a practice to frequently observe your group in action so that you can more accurately assess your true leader/member relationships. Specifically, there are two major components to look for:

■ *The support you get from your reps.* Do they do what you want them to do in a timely fashion with a minimum of reluctance and grumbling?

■ *The relationships among the various members of your sales team.* Is it harmonious, or is there conflict and dissension?

How well the group and its leader get along is the foundation of all good leader/member relationships and is reflected in individual accomplishment, organizational morale, and employee turnover.*

Truly effective sales leaders earn the respect of their reps by treating them with dignity and satisfying their psychological needs. They strive for a felicitous equilibrium between the needs of their individual salespeople and the needs of the company. This is indeed a most delicate balancing act because each rep seeks freedom and creativity in his or her work, while most business organizations are built upon control and a certain amount of conformity. Therein lies your foremost leadership challenge. You're caught between a rock and a hard spot.

The first step in managing mavericks is to understand their sometimes rebellious nature and develop a healthy tolerance for their unique and unorthodox behavior. Even though you are the boss, they still might not listen to you or follow your lead. Is this really that important if they are your top order producers? If they are marginal producers or underachievers, however, that is an entirely different matter.

Your next step is to select the management power style which is most appropriate for their needs at their particular stages of development. The maturity and competence levels of your reps must be factored into the leadership equation. Depending upon the situation and the species of rep, your management style can range from one that provides an environment in which your range riders are tightly controlled to one in which they are given as much latitude as possible to perform their jobs as they see fit. Your task now becomes the manipulation of each maverick in terms of his or her psychological personality profile and innovative selling style to create win-win scenarios for all.

*Material adapted from Fred E. Fiedler, *A Theory of Leadership Effectiveness,* McGraw-Hill, New York, 1967.

How to Manage the Affiliator/Pleaser Maverick

Because these reps are driven by recognition needs, friendship and goodwill are the best ways to relate to them. Give them plenty of strokes and reassurance. When coaching, use directive and reflective questions to guide them into doing what you want them to do. They have a sincere and compelling desire to please you but also want to be "part of the gang." Peer pressure can thus be used to bring them into line or to do tough assignments — like paperwork — which they detest.

Utilize their God-given talents in a manner that is mutually beneficial for this fun-loving individual and the organization. For example, affiliators are expert conflict-resolution agents, great at building and maintaining relationships while keeping morale high. Their enthusiasm can be infectious and bridge emotional gaps during and after a crisis. They are excellent compromisers and fence-menders but crave constant attention and appreciation while thriving on gossip.

Affiliators are superb at client maintenance, public relations, and entertaining at conventions and sales meetings and extremely effective as project leaders for team selling efforts. Since they aren't particularly good at planning, detail work, or reports, they could be relieved of these responsibilities in favor of more freewheeling duties where their outgoing personalities and innate creativity can flourish unabated. Keep them away from technical accounts, routine selling situations, and clients who won't appreciate their brand of jokes.

Although they are relatively easy to manage, affiliator/pleasers are not particularly loyal to you or your firm. They want to do what's popular and feel part of the team but tend to be fickle. Power boss sales managers often bully their affiliator reps and withhold recognition, knowing that these insecure salespeople will do anything to keep the peace and please the boss. These tactics work well in the short run but are not as effective as continuous recognition, public praise, and frequent pats on the back.

How to Manage the Power Boss/Commander Maverick

The same way that porcupines make love — *carefully!* This is the toughest personality management challenge for newly appointed sales managers. If poorly handled, a PB/C maverick, like a mad bull in a china shop, can wreck your sales department and ruin your management career. With a little moxie and a lot of nerve, you can turn these macho gunslingers into your most powerful organizational weapon.

Since power boss reps have tremendous ego needs and usually perceive strength as competence, you must always ride tall in the saddle and be very decisive when interfacing with them. Be direct, whip butt, and provide options and alternatives—*your* options and *your* alternatives. Let them decide what to do and how to do it. Allow them to take the credit—even if the account strategy was your idea and not theirs. Let them "win," satisfy their overwhelming need to be right, stroke their elephantine egos, and above all, *give them a challenge.* Power people have a compelling need to prove to you, themselves, and apparently the whole world how great they are. Underneath their fierce facade lurks an insecure human being.

You can play upon this basic insecurity with devastating effectiveness by manipulating them into taking on the toughest territory, the "impossible" customers, and the dirtiest jobs. Throwing down the achievement gauntlet will stimulate these action-oriented gauchos to do the impossible for you on a continuing basis. Once you get over your fear of them and reverse the intimidation process, power boss reps can be easily manipulated and transformed into most loyal and dependable employees.

Sure, you're going to have your share of confrontations, complete with temper tantrums and simulated shoot-outs, so you will want to give them lots of space. This is a bucking bronco that you break in hard and fast and then ride lightly ever after. Whenever they succeed, laud them lavishly in public, but when they fail, come down hard on them—in private. Let them know who's the boss, that they're in a tough outfit, and that you're going to be looking right down their throats. Remember, they need the job more than you need them. Although a manipulator/facilitator rep would probably smile at these statements, a PB/C rep would quickly shape up. You see, they *expect* you to be tough, or they won't ever respect you. Strength and power are the only things that count with them. Everything else, including scientific management, is sheer weakness.

What kind of job assignments turn power boss salespersons on? Cold calling, new account development, troubleshooting situations, and an occasional leadership role in your sales meetings or training sessions. These tasks enable them to show off their fantastic selling skills and share their awesome sales experiences with admiring audiences. They instill a healthy competitive spirit in every successful sales organization. God love 'em!

When coaching PB/Cs, use nondirective and reflective questions to subtly guide their thinking. Being quick on the draw, they would rather talk than listen, and they have very short attention spans. Therefore, you must come quickly to the point when coaching, counseling, or evaluating their performances. Sandwich blunt criticism between heavy layers of praise. Never reassure them, but when the chips are down, appeal to their pride and ego needs. Applying peer pressure can also be effective in shaping their intuitive behavior.

Above-average order-producing power boss reps with consistently good performance records should be given more freedom of action than most of your other salespeople. Give these horses their heads and watch them run! These trailblazers can be a real inspiration to the rest of your sales force.

How to Manage the Avoider/Abdicator Maverick

Look to the future. Begin by evaluating their long-term contributions to your organization. What are their order-producing potentials? Because you will be compelled to invest more time and energy in developing these reps into successful salespeople than all of the other four personality types combined, you must decide up front whether they have the capabilities of making it. Since there are opportunity costs involved as well as your precious time and energy, you must either fire them now — cut your losses — or prepare yourself for a long-term siege.

If you perceive enough performance potential to warrant your intensive involvement, your best bet is to adopt a nonthreatening, anxiety-reducing management style which removes all threats, intimidations, and confrontations. Give them lots of reassurance and precise directions. They need it. You must be exceedingly patient and continually satisfy the avoider's needs for security and predictability. If you give them a list of accounts with the names, titles, and locations of each buying influence to call upon in their territories on a regular basis, they will feel more comfortable. Providing them with a structured, or "canned pitch," sales presentation and lots of technical data will give them even more confidence.

Critique your avoiders before and after each day's work, if possible, and tell them exactly what to do and when. Focus on minor points and use directive questions as you guide them through each troubled step of the way. Learn to mumble with the best of them and watch the volume level of your voice. In the beginning, don't give them any challenging assignments, such as cold-calling, creating dealer cooperative advertising programs, or conducting distributor training sessions. Rewriting the sales manual or market research activities are good nonthreatening starters. The closer that these timid tyros can stick to a tried-and-true routine, the better they will feel, and the better they will perform. Motivated by security and physiological (survival on the job) needs, their prime modus operandi is to preserve the status quo and to avoid as much contact with their clientele — and you — as possible.

These salespeople are your average order producers, and whether you like them or not, no sales organization can survive without them. They provide a steadying influence on the other team members and create continuity from one sales manager to the next. If you really work hard on their professional development, you will be pleasantly surprised to find that some avoiders can be nurtured into becoming your most loyal and productive team members. They don't like change and sometimes stay on the job forever. These are the survivors of every organization.

Dumbo, the Salesperson

An interesting perspective on the effective management of avoider/abdicator mavericks is provided by the story of Dumbo the Elephant. As you will recall, Dumbo had huge ears and a little mouse friend who claimed that the big mammal could fly in the circus, if he held a little red feather in his trunk. "You can fly," the mouse insisted, "if you flap your ears and hang on tightly to this little red feather." Dumbo *believed* him and learned to fly, becoming a big hit at the local circus. One day while aloft, however, he sneezed and let go of the feather. When he saw it floating down to the ground below, the elephant got so excited that he started flapping his ears very fast. This created an air cushion which supported his flight. When he didn't fall, Dumbo realized that it wasn't the red feather that enabled him to fly, it was his own ability, his big ears.

And that is precisely your job as developer of Dumbo salespeople. Give them all of the red feathers that you can to support their progress. As they become more assured, you gradually start withdrawing this temporary support system until they learn to do it themselves. Sure, some will crash and burn, but those who respond to your efforts on their behalf will soon realize, as Dumbo did, that they can succeed in selling because of their own abilities. These reps will never forget your thoughtful attention to their professional welfare by helping them develop their self-confidence and selling skills. Do you think that you would ever lose these salespeople to a competitor for a few hundred extra bucks a week? No way, José! This is the stuff that long-term relationships are made of. If he or she can make quota, you've got a loyal team member for life. Just be careful that you don't get stuck with a bunch of Dum-dum avoider reps who can't sell and won't quit!

From Wimp to Winner

In summary, you can develop avoiders into achievers if you create trust by accepting them as they are and helping them understand their own personalities. Make them feel psychologically safe, encourage them to set goals, and give them the tools to do the job. Be patient, and encourage them to try to change. When they are paralyzed with fear of failure, ask them, "What is the worst thing that can happen if you proceed?" When they start answering, "I could get better," you know that favorable change is imminent. These are some of the things that you can do to get avoider/abdicators to want to change. There is no greater job satisfaction than knowing that you are directly responsible for their growth and development into winners. You are a positive agent of change, a real awareness catalyst. You reflect back to them what they are and what they are capable of becoming.

How to Manage the Achiever/Technician Maverick

These Lone Rangers are stimulated by pride and self-actualization needs while deriving a sense of fulfillment from challenging field selling assignments. They thrive on data and only respect other bright people, such as fellow "techies" and manipulators, while dismissing affiliators as lightweights and avoiders as losers. They relate worst of all to power bosses, who violate their needs for self-reliance, spontaneity, and creativity. These frustrations cause much conflict between these two strong personality types.

You can play upon this interpersonal tension by setting up a friendly rivalry with their fellow PB/C sales team members and by challenging them to do the impossible—often. Both personality types will respond with great enthusiasm and perhaps ignite the rest of the team to keep up with them. You know that achievers are not going to allow those brain-dead cowpunchers to outachieve them in anything. By the same token, power bosses aren't going to allow those propeller-head number-crunchers to show them up. Now you've started a game of "can you top this?" Set them up, turn them on, and watch them go!

When managing achiever reps, you can adopt a range of manipulative tactics which will constantly challenge and stretch these hard-working individuals. They perform best on tasks that *they* feel are important and meaningful, permit learning, and allow them to be independent and resourceful. Play upon achiever pride. Coax them to share their vast knowledge with others. Give them leadership roles, and above all, create an exciting, competitive atmosphere.

Offer these energetic go-getters short-range payoffs, and have them working on several difficult tasks at the same time. They are splendid project people who thrive on hard work and problem solving. Involve them in outside field training, market reconnaissance, and territory analysis as well as sales meeting planning and leadership. Provide them with a constant flow of facts and figures while using reflective and nondirective questions to guide them along. Because they are extremely efficient in their work habits, particularly excelling in time and territory management, you should solicit their valuable input for the benefit of your other sales team members as frequently as possible. Although they will never admit it, their team contributions are also good for their egos.

If you can gain the respect of achievers as a knowledgeable and professional sales leader, they will move mountains for you. Under your expert tutelage, achievers can develop human and conceptual skills. When that happens, they've "graduated" to manipulator/facilitator status. Failing to provide them with challenging and mind-stretching assignments, however, will cause immediate boredom and eventual defection to another company. If you play this personality right, they will be the backbone of your organization and one of the prime reasons for your success.

How to Manage the Manipulator/Facilitator Maverick

Although *all* levels of Maslow's Hierarchy of Human Needs are factored into the manipulator/facilitator behavior equation, the need for self-actualization appears to be dominant. Early in the game you must identify these strategic thinkers and either eliminate this future competition or make them your personal protégés. Find out what their long-range game plans are—why are they here and what do they want?—and then show them that by using your sales job opportunity (under your guidance and direction, of course), they will be able to reach those lofty career objectives and get what they want.

This requires a great deal of preparation, listening, and observing on your part. Your task here is to accumulate as much information from every possible source, both inside and outside your firm, so that you can understand exactly who and what you are dealing with. When interacting with them, use reflective and nondirective questions to draw them out and gauge your relationship. If it's *your* job that they desire, then you can start grooming your successor. If it's your *boss's* job that they covet, you may need their friendship and support later on. By showing them positive results for their long-range objectives, you are creating a win-win working situation which should assure you of their continuous cooperation.

During the course of this mutually beneficial interpersonal relationship, you will most likely become engaged in a series of negotiations and game-playing situations, but that comes with the territory. Be strong, always do the unexpected, never forget who's the boss, and you will keep the upper hand in this most stimulating relationship.

Teach them almost everything that you know, while exposing them to each facet of your business. Delegate many management responsibilities to these alert people, and gradually introduce them to various leadership roles. Become their mentor. Manipulator/facilitators are the real "comers" on your staff, the truly bright and ambitious ones. If you earn their respect, you will have the most loyal lieutenants that any sales manager could ever hope for. With a little luck, you will be able to find and develop your fair share of these exceptional people.

On Developing New Mavericks

Before you hired this new salesperson, you had her territory and sold over 1000 units on an annual basis. Because of your range-riding experience, you feel that its real market potential is 1500 units. That's why you relinquished this turf and brought in this greenhorn. Unfortunately, she is unskilled, untrained, and scared stiff. This rookie does not think that she could sell more than 300 units during the first full year. What do you do?

It is obvious that you and your new rep do not see things the same way because of something called perceptual double vision. You are confronted with two vastly different views—yours (based on first-hand knowledge and selling experience) and hers (founded upon fear, inexperience, and immaturity). Like the biblical maverick Moses, you see beyond the desert to the promised land, while your new rep, like his newly freed followers, sees only the burning sands and possible starvation. Moses' vision extended beyond the immediate obstacles to the larger, overall objective, whereas his subordinates were mainly preoccupied with immediate, short-term problems—which seemed overwhelming. Your leadership task here is similar to Moses' mandate. You must broaden your reps' vision and expand their horizons of accomplishment while stretching their capacity for personal growth and development.

Returning to our little scenario, how do you handle this frightened newcomer? You can't simply order her to sell 1000 units. That won't work. If persuasion won't do it, then you must *negotiate* her sales goals in a sequential manner. After much heated discussion and counterpersuasion, you finally compromise, settling on a quota of 500 units to to be sold in her territory during the forthcoming year. Then *you both sign a sales quota agreement.* Now, are either of you happy with this compromise agreement? Probably not. You've asked her to do 40 percent more than she thought she could do, and you are settling for 50 percent, or half of what you know can be done in the territory.

The year passes and upon its conclusion your new rep has sold exactly 500 units in her sales territory. On a scale of 1 to 100, how do you rate her job performance? *Answer:* You've got to give her a 100 percent rating because she accomplished her goal. Remember, like it or not, you both signed off on that 500-unit figure.

Next year, however, you will renegotiate her quota to 700 or 800 units because she has gained more experience and self-confidence while you are stretching her closer to your long-term territorial order-production goal. As she continues to make progress you will encourage her to reach new plateaus of 900, 1200, and eventually 1500 annual unit sales. With patience, encouragement, training, and coaching, you can help this new salesperson and all of your other mavericks to reach their promised land of quota attainment and commission earnings.

Hercules became the strongest man in the world by carrying a newborn calf on his shoulders for one mile each day until it was a full-grown cow. If he had tried to pick up the adult cow without this kind of intensive preparation, its weight would have injured him. Your objective in developing your subordinates is to strengthen their vocational muscles not to give them an occupational hernia.

Step-by-step, you guide them to new heights of accomplishment. Throughout this stretching and strengthening process, they are keenly aware of your facilitating efforts and know that a long-term association with your leadership will be most beneficial to their professional growth and development. That's how to build a viable sales organization.

Sales Force Management Summary

Mature, responsible mavericks such as achievers, manipulators, and some power bosses require a loosely controlled, flexible organization with general supervision in order to reach their full selling potential. Immature, inexperienced, and untrained salespeople and some avoiders and affiliators need a structured organization with more individual attention and personal interaction with you in order to develop their selling talents. The hallmark of effective sales executives is the ability to adapt their management styles to the various personalities of their team members, giving them meaningful job assignments which will simultaneously satisfy those individual agendas and organizational objectives.

Chapter 11 Roundup

This chapter presented suggestions for managing mavericks, avoiding demotivational traps, and building a winning sales team. The truly effective sales manager provides challenging work assignments and satisfies the psychological needs of her or his salespeople. Such managers are skillful at developing each individual team member—regardless of his or her maturity or experiential levels—and shaping his or her behavior within an organizational context. Sales managers must manage by manipulating their mavericks in win-win scenarios.

PART 4

The End of the Trail

God, give us grace to accept with serenity the things that cannot be changed, courage to change the things which should be changed, and the wisdom to distinguish the one from the other.   REINHOLD NIEBUHR

12
The Code of the Old West

Aways do the right thing in the right way.
ANONYMOUS COWPOKE

Introduction to Power and Ethics

The Code of the Old West is concerned with the dynamics of power and how you — the newly appointed sales manager — use it to attain the legitimate goals of your organization. Ethical issues regarding counseling, appraising, and terminating mavericks are also discussed in this final chapter.

Position Power

Position power is the possession of control, authority, and influence that an executive has over others by virtue of occupying a particular leadership position in an organizational hierarchy. It is the amount of latitude that you have to reward and punish your subordinates. *Power* is the ability to impose your will on others, whether they like it or not. It is also the capacity to make the flow of events go in the direction you wish. Power assumes one of two forms: power *over* and power to *act*. Enlightened sales management is concerned with using power to inspire concerted team action toward the attainment of organizational objectives.

Bases of Power

The psychologists John R. French, Jr., and Bertram Raven have discovered five power sources which each leader possesses in varying degrees.* (Your attitude and leadership behavior can modify or enhance each of these bases of power.)

1. *Reward power.* The ability to provide monetary, social, political, or psychological rewards to others for compliance to your directives. This is your capacity to recompense work well done, provide perks, or offer favorable job assignments to cooperative sales team members.

2. *Coercive power.* The ability to provide monetary or other punishments for noncompliance. This is your right to penalize errant reps, discipline them, or threaten their job security.

3. *Attraction power.* The ability to elicit compliance from others because they like you. This is sometimes called charisma and is an underlying factor in establishing and maintaining good leader/member relationships because innate human skills are required to gain group acceptance and collaboration.

4. *Expert power.* The ability to gain group cooperation because of technical expertise, either actual or reputed. This is created by your previous selling track record and current administrative capabilities — the task structure of your job.

5. *Status power.* The ability to gain cooperation because of a legitimate position of power in a company. This is usually based upon your position in the firm and your job description.

Power and Leadership

The most important leadership trait which distinguishes successful from unsuccessful sales managers is that the successful ones are primarily motivated by their desire to possess power. This is not surprising: power facilitates team member cooperation because mavericks just nat-

---

*This material was derived from the research of John R. French, Jr., and Bertram Raven, "The Bases of Social Power," in D. Cartwright (ed.), *Studies in Social Power,* University of Michigan Press, Ann Arbor, 1959, pp. 150–167.

urally work more readily for those who have organizational "pull" and know what they are doing. Just as earnestly, they will sabotage those who do not. Remember, the world will stand aside for people who look and act like they know what they're doing. Are you one of those bold people?

Although position power is the aspect of situational control which usually comes to mind first, it is the *least important* of the three components of leadership control and influence over a sales force. Many newly appointed sales managers erroneously believe, however, that it's easy to be a boss if you have lots of power to reward and punish subordinates, that the job title speaks for itself, causing your reps to automatically fall into line. They say, "You give me the authority, and there's no way I won't be in command." This is a most naive view of something as complex as leadership. If your mavericks don't like you or your management style, they will surely "do you in," regardless of how much power you have. Among other things, they will withhold their support during times of crisis and then wear you down in the long run with passive resistance.

While power is officially conferred by the firm, the real clout of sales managers is derived from their staff's willingness to accept their authority. If you can get your recommendations accepted and your salespeople promoted or get them desirable assignments, your power in their eyes will be higher than if you have little or no influence with your own boss. That's why you must build good leader/member relationships upward as well as downward.

Furthermore, your consistent leadership role behavior will give you *referent power*—the desire of subordinates to emulate you. Once you have reached this level in your leader/member relationships, your organizational power base will be both awesome and secure and your actions will carry much conviction and decisiveness. Now you *know* that you're going to last more than four years on the job.

Modifying Your Position Power

Who but a damned fool or a poet would want to do that? Most new sales managers are at a strategic disadvantage, so they would want to increase their position power at once. They need to quickly establish an organizational power base and obtain compliance from their new subordinates. As they gain more control over their job and team member behavior, lowering their position power and making other adjustments might be warranted. In the beginning, however, the pursuit of power and control are absolute necessities for survival.

To increase your position power, you can immediately make a show of your power: become, as rapidly as possible, an expert on the job and make sure that information to your group gets channeled through you. To manage information is to manage change, and at the moment, you are the prime change agent in your company. You manage the only revenue-producing function of your firm, and you have the pulse of its marketplace. Extra training programs, university extension classes, and current books on sales management will shorten your learning curve and enable you to become an expert on the job. Sir Francis Bacon said that "knowledge is power," and nowhere is that more true than in managing mavericks. Hiring, firing, penalizing, disciplining, transferring, and reassignment to desirable or less-desirable territories are weapons which you have at your disposal to assert your authority and show your new sales force "who's the boss."

The Cleveland Massacre

Fully exercising the inherent powers of your position can also have a devastating downside effect on your leader/member relationships. An insecure sales manager who shall go unnamed learned this lesson the hard way. While conducting the midwestern states segment of a companywide training program in Cleveland, he became incensed with the passive resistance of this half of his sales force and suddenly fired everyone in the hotel meeting room! Did he get their attention? Did he establish himself as leader of the pack? Certainly.

Now that the herd was properly chastised and subdued, he allowed them to reapply for their jobs within the next 30 days. He and his regional sales managers would then decide who was to be reemployed. It was a dramatic way of making his point, the sales manager gloated, but it proved to be a costly and shortsighted victory. Within a year, all of his good salespeople and best regional managers had left the company. He really showed everyone who was the boss!

Power, Ambition, and Manipulation

Henry Kissinger said that "power is the great aphrodisiac" and this has caused many a leader's untimely fall from grace. Lord Acton observed that "power tends to corrupt and absolute power corrupts absolutely." These are pretty dim views of the most driving force in effective leadership in the modern business world. Lord Macaulay put it in proper perspective when he asserted, "The highest proof of virtue is to possess boundless power without abusing it." These are the sentiments behind the manipulator/facilitator win-win philosophy which has been advocated throughout this book. Power, ambition, and manipulation are positive forces and mandatory prerequisites for long-term success in sales management. When properly channeled, they enable sales managers to achieve a harmonious balance between the needs of the individual and the needs of the organization.

Ambition, that compelling desire to succeed, lies at the very core of leadership. All business organizations require sales executives who are impelled by it to direct the energy of salespeople and tap their full potential. It is this overwhelming urge to gain ever-increasing amounts of money, power, and responsibility which marks a successful sales leader. When shared ambition becomes embedded in a corporate culture, it generates near-invincible power. It becomes a creative and benign force for the attainment of organizational objectives. If ambition is self-serving and individualized, however, it can destroy the company. Many contemporary examples abound.

Finally, the last leadership misconception — manipulation: Ever since the days of Niccolò Machiavelli this term has suggested duplicity and deceit, leaders who value ends over means in achieving their nefarious purposes. Let's explode this management myth once and for all. We are not uttering negatives; we are talking about the creation of positive, win-win situations in which *all* parties — the company, its employees, customers, stockholders, suppliers, and society — benefit from the relationship. Certainly many of these suggested methods can be used for self-serving and potentially damaging purposes, but that is where professionalism and morality enter the leadership equation.

Your goal is not to ascend the company organizational hierarchy, moving from one management responsibility to another, while your former department collapses like a house of cards after you are gone. No, the name of the manipulation management game is to leave behind you a situation in which common sense, without the grace of your presence, can reign with success. We are not speaking about raw power and ambition per se but the overall business success that they both can engender.

Counseling, Evaluating, and Terminating Mavericks

Everything that you do in sales management has ethical implications which reveal your true character. Nowhere else is the use of your position power more exposed than in the counseling, appraising, and termination of your mavericks.

Counseling is professional guidance of individual salespeople through the use of psychological techniques and the offering of advice and direction. Sometimes the most competent and experienced range riders will falter in the line of duty and exhibit failing performance, particularly when immersed in the throes of a prolonged selling slump.

The purpose of counseling is to discover the *real* reason, or problem, that is blocking their endeavors in the field. It is designed to improve selling skills and overall performance levels. Sometimes your mavericks have psychological "blocks" which they are either unaware of or are reluctant to admit. Those mind-sets and thought patterns which inhibit productivity are called motivational blocks. Your task is to identify and remove those achievement obstacles and get your reps back on track.

Up to this point, you have provided training, coaching, and technical support to all of your salespeople. Although you have given them the tools to do their jobs, certain individuals are not performing up to expectations or previously established standards. Why? There are several distinct possibilities: you might have hired the wrong person or failed to adequately train and support him or her, or there might be something else. That something else is what you are after in the counseling sessions.

An impending or recent divorce; alcohol or drug addiction; emotional, financial, or health problems; and burnout are all reasons for poor or declining job performance. Needless to say, professional help might be needed to get these employees back in the saddle. People can improve if they want to improve. Not everyone, however, is salvageable. Now you're confronted with a moral dilemma: *What do you do with these poor, unfortunate souls?* Do you fire them, or do you retain them? Let your conscience and the needs of the organization be your guides.

Your counseling activities should set the stage for frank and open discussions regarding the problems which have been identified and possible solutions and courses of action. If it is an area that does not require psychiatric help or substance-abuse rehabilitation programs, you should get the problem maverick to lay out a timetable, with periodic benchmarks of progress, toward mutually acceptable goals. Often this step-by-step approach, under your patient and understanding supervision, will enable the errant rep to regain confidence and return to form. If not, sterner measures might have to be taken and the documentation process started. Remember, you're a sales manager, not a social worker.

The Harvey Blue Case Revisited

Newly appointed sales managers would be well advised to begin their tenure in office by scheduling a series of private meetings with each of their mavericks. In handling the old-time salesperson or disgruntled veteran—like Harvey Blue in our Chap. 4 case study, who thought that he should have gotten *your* promotion—an immediate counseling session is in order. Discretion and forbearance are required because all of your new subordinates must be quickly won over but on your terms.

In the case of the Harvey Blues—power contenders within the ranks—you begin by showing respect for their years of valuable service to the company and express interest in building a mutually beneficial relationship. Then tell them in a firm voice: "I had little to do with getting my new assignment, but now that I have the job, I want to do it well. Perhaps you could do the job even better, but that is not what Management wanted, or I wouldn't be here now. They selected me — not you. Those are the facts.

"My success depends upon how helpful I can be to you and the other members of this sales team. I want a chance to work with you, profit from your excellent experience, and perhaps bring you some ideas which will help you to do even better and derive more satisfaction from your present position."

Usually this low-key method of laying down the law works well and a potentially explosive personnel problem is defused. Occasionally the recalcitrant older salesperson, sexist subordinate, or disillusioned veteran will still refuse to cooperate. Then you will have to consider disciplinary measures, transfer, or ultimately, termination. You're the boss; let none forget it!

The Appraisal Process

A fair and accurate evaluation of your mavericks' job performances is a critical but time-consuming task. The purposes of performance appraisal conferences are to discuss your salespeople's progress, isolate areas which need improvement, and help them develop corrective plans that will enable them to reach goals that they aren't presently attaining.

Set aside your personal feelings regarding each sales team member and be as objective as possible when interfacing with them. Your attitude toward them and these confidential conferences will determine your effectiveness in conducting these sessions, their outcome, and the general morale of your entire sales force. After thorough preparation and review of a particular rep's performance record to date, you should be positive and matter-of-fact, saying, in effect, "This is where you are now, and this is where you are *supposed* to be. These are your options. Let's review your strengths and weaknesses so that we can set some meaningful goals together."

This approach picks up the thread from your original hiring interview session, when you told the serious candidates what the sales position required in term of order production, territorial coverage, and administrative responsibilities. It also validates the quota which you both negotiated and reestablishes your forceful and consistent leadership. Not only are you helping your mavericks plan but you're demonstrating *consistency of purpose* as well as continued interest in their professional welfare.

Select Realistic and Fair Bases
for Evaluation

As much as possible, quantitative criteria should be used in preference to qualitative ones. Quantitative evaluation factors include anything that you can hang a number on, such as sales volume, gross margin by product line, customer group, order size, number of accounts, calls per day, days worked, direct selling expense, and selling time versus nonselling time. Qualitative factors include product knowledge, time and territory management, personal appearance and health, customer relations, personality, attitude, and self-improvement programs.

Subjective methods, such as executive judgment and management opinion, leave much to be desired because personal biases tend to distort the ratings. There should be clear-cut goals and objective evaluation criteria. In summary, appraisal of your mavericks is crucial not only because pay increases and promotions should be based on such ratings but because good supervision and training should be predicated on a fair evaluation of each rep's performance. There can be no halo or horns effects here. Too much—including your job future—depends upon it.

The Firing Line: Terminations Are the Test

The "firing line" is perhaps the most acute test of a sales manager's character. *Who* gets fired, *why* they get fired, *how* they get fired, and *when*, goes to the very heart and soul of sales management leadership. Terminations are the test of your professionalism, revealing your character and value system in the process.

Unfortunately, there will always be some mavericks in your outfit who simply do not want to work. They are the "prairie dogs," who lie down on the job and give selling a bad name. Everyone else in your sales force knows who they are and what they are not doing. Although these individuals are shirking their full field responsibilities, nobody is going to step forward to tell you. "Squealing" on a fellow maverick goes against the Code of the Old West. Instead, they will all be watching you, waiting to see what—if anything—you're going to do. Once again, your leadership is on the line.

Quite frankly, your course of action is obvious. It's your duty to recognize these loafers and promptly get rid of them before their attitude infects your entire organization. And when you finally fire them, you'll earn the admiration and respect of all of your hardworking and productive mavericks who have long resented these freeloaders in their ranks. Only then will the others come forward and comment. They had all been wondering how long you were going to put up with this situation before you took decisive action. Thus, terminating subordinates can be a constructive act. It tends to clear the air, reinforces the work ethic, reestablishes your authority, and improves the motivational climate.

Termination Procedure

If termination isn't practiced as a procedure, it will always be a problem. The termination procedure actually begins during the selection process where job requirements are communicated to serious applicants. The job description spells out duties and responsibilities, while annual sales quotas are either assigned or negotiated.

Each new employee is then indoctrinated and assimilated into the organization. Intensive product and selling-skills training provides these newcomers with the tools to do the job. Outside training and coaching in the field should further enhance their ability to perform up to expectations. The "can do" factors of their qualifications and prior selling experience are now about to be translated into "will do" and organizational fit factors. You've given them the tools and the support system to do the job, and now it is up to them to return a substantial sales volume dividend for your investment in their development. They've got to earn their keep.

Somewhere down the road it may become apparent that some of your new mavericks either will not perform or don't fit into your company culture. This is the time for counseling. The real reasons for nonperformance or noncompliance must be jointly identified and addressed. An improvement program—where warranted—must be established with sequential benchmarks and mutually agreed-upon objectives and timetables.

At this critical juncture the documentation procedure begins in case disciplinary action is required; your firing decisions cannot be whimsical or arbitrary. The Equal Employment Opportunity Commission might require you to defend your actions in a court of law. As you know, without hard evidence of incompetency or nonperformance, the courts tend to favor the "little guy" over the large, monolithic, unfeeling company.

When you are absolutely certain that a marginal maverick has had all of the training and support to do the job but still won't make it, you must give that maverick the pink slip and let him or her out to pasture. Don't hesitate; delays only make matters worse and ultimately cause hard feelings. Do it as decently as possible, and if you can, bend the severance pay rules in his or her favor as much as possible, while allowing the rep to retain a sense of dignity. Remember, you have a reputation to protect, and the word does get around the range pretty quickly. Sometimes yesterday's employee can become tomorrow's customer. Under

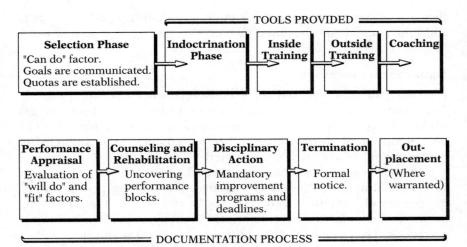

Figure 12-1. The termination procedure legally begins when you hire new mavericks and concludes when they have left the firm. Under exceptional circumstances, deserving individuals are either given early retirement or assistance in obtaining employment with other companies. This procedure recognizes the needs of both the individual and the firm.

certain special circumstances—such as the termination of a longtime, loyal, or former "star" salesperson with seniority—the services of a professional outplacement firm could be retained to enable these deserving individuals to obtain employment with minimum disruption of their careers. Figure 12-1 illustrates the termination procedure.

The Moral Hazards of Sales Management

How do you reconcile and integrate concern for the individual with concern for the organization when conflicts of these interests exist? Especially when your boss is on your back for immediate results? These are the ethical issues which every sales manager must, sooner or later, come to grips with. They stem from the pluralism of value systems in our society.

Most of us have been raised to believe in the Judeo-Christian aphorisms that one must love thy neighbor as thyself, blessed are the meek, and brotherly love should rule the world. Yet in the business world one encounters such attitudes as competition is good, the company can't afford to be its brother's keeper, take care of Number One, and power produces results. Thus, if you are chosen to lead or manage others — and if you carefully review your daily activities — you are bound to be perplexed by these two conflicting value systems. Yes, you believe in free will and individualism — those fine Jeffersonian precepts — yet within your firm, conformity is fostered and to a certain degree admired. For example, to be labeled a "good company man or woman" is usually considered a sign of high esteem and approval. Mavericks are singled out early in the game and watched with great suspicion by their peers and superiors. And here you are, a manager of mavericks, and perhaps a little mavericky yourself. Can you afford to buck the system by using your position power sparingly, giving these renegades their freedom to ride roughshod in their territories as they see fit? Or do you rein them in, tightly controlling their endeavors, and thereby stifling all creative growth and development? In your mad dash to "beat last year's numbers," you could forget that individual initiative, team effort, and morality are the foundations of your success in sales management.

Ethical Dilemmas

Consider the following dilemmas. Then check Chap. 13, "The Sales Manager's Manual," if there are any answers you are unsure of.

Case 1. Your boss, the owner of a recreational vehicle manufacturing firm, dislikes and distrusts one of your mavericks and wants him fired. Fearing that your rep will ride off into the sunset with the $50,000 recreational vehicle model which he presently drives around the territory, the boss has a "special termination plan" that he wants you to become party to. Noting that this maverick's travel itinerary includes a visit to your largest Baltimore dealer this week, your boss directs you to do the following:

- Telephone your big dealer now, telling him that when your salesperson arrives on his premises that you want to talk to him. The rep should call you at once.
- While your rep is on the phone with you, the dealer is to immediately impound the RV.
- Then you are to fire the rep on the spot.

What do you think of your boss's "special termination plan"? How will you handle it? This is a tough case, because you could arouse the wrath of the owner if you refuse to follow his directives and wind up losing your own job in the process. Was there anything wrong with the rep's performance? Is this merely a case of personality conflict, or is this maverick not doing the job? Another factor to be considered is your relationship with your boss, the company owner. Who's really running the sales show, he or you? If this kind of interference in your area of authority is typical, then perhaps you're in the wrong place and should move on. Obviously, his "special termination plan" stinks and should be disregarded. Make up your résumé, because he's probably got an even more "special termination plan" for you!

Case 2.   Can you afford to be loyal to former classmates, business associates, or old friends in the company? When they can't cut it anymore or fail to perform up to company standards, how do you handle them?

Case 3.   How long should you put up with alcoholic or drug-addicted subordinates? Before you respond, consider the well-known unwritten Code of the Old West which states "Always support your mavericks." Does it apply in these two cases?

Case 4.   Your boss orders you to fire a maverick while the latter is either away on vacation or ill in the hospital. If you ever even think of doing such a dastardly deed, I suggest you reconsider. How many times have you heard horror stories about salespeople returning from extended tours of their territories only to find the locks on their company office doors changed, their furniture lying on the front lawn, and their personal effects wrapped up neatly in a sealed plastic bag? In today's impersonal business environment, there are many marginal mavericks who are afraid to take vacations because they think that they might not have a job left when they return.

Is this the way to run a ranch? Are these ruthless deeds consistent with respect for the dignity of human beings, morality in management, or the team-building concept? *No!* This is manipulation management at its self-serving worst, whether done in the name of company, duty, or efficiency. Somehow, *we must reconcile and integrate concern for the individual with concern for the organization.* To place one above the other spells moral disaster. They are both vital to business and society and exist in a system of mutual causality.

The Morality Index

Figure 12-2 graphically illustrates this leadership dilemma and a range of possible interactions between them. The horizontal axis indicates concern for the organization, while the vertical axis shows concern for the individual. The Morality Index can also be related to Fig. 2-2, the psychological profiling of mavericks, because we are dealing with executive attitudes and value systems.

When comparing the two grids, you can see the following interrela-

Figure 12-2. The Morality Index.

tionships and complementary factors. The upper left-hand quadrant contains the affiliator/pleaser sales managers, who encourage their individual mavericks to do their own thing, often trading control for popularity and group acceptance. The opposite philosophy is espoused by the power boss/commander sales managers, who would repress individual initiative to organizational goals. The middle, or compromise, position on the Index is occupied by the achiever/technicians, who advocate individual freedom of action but also recognize the necessity for group collaboration.

Avoider/abdicator sales managers, who lurk in the lower left-hand quadrant, are strictly out for themselves. They eschew both individual and company goals in favor of their own secret ambitions. Although manipulator/facilitator sales managers view business as a game—to be won at any cost—they strive for a mutually beneficial balance between the needs of their individual mavericks and the needs of their firms. That's why they are located in the upper right-hand quadrant of the Morality Index. The ethical ones have a sincere desire to construct win-win scenarios, where *everyone* benefits from playing the sales management game *their* way.

As a moral manager, you should opt for that upper right-hand corner on the Morality Index. But is this always possible when dealing with the harsh realities of your job? Unforeseeable circumstances and strong personalities will test the strength of your moral fiber. Outrages will be perpetrated in the name of cost-cutting; character assassinations and the use of "dirty tricks" are becoming increasingly a part of organizational life. Consider our last two ethical dilemmas.

Case 5. What about inefficient old-timers? Do you fire them or do you carry this deadwood on your payroll? You're damned if you do and damned if you don't. In either case, what do you tell the other sales team members? How do you justify your decision? And what kind of messages are you sending out to the entire organization?

Case 6. Or consider the related case of your former "star" salesperson who has faithfully served your company well for several decades and is now in failing health and declining ability. This burned-out maverick is only a few years away from retirement. What do you do with him or her? In the name of cost-efficiency, do you throw the baggage out? Or, in the name of humanity, do you look the other way? The ethical ball is now squarely in your court.

These are some of the tougher moral issues which will confront you during your continual quest for increased sales and organizational effectiveness. How much human wreckage will be strewn along your path to managerial success? These are the moral hazards of sales management which can ultimately debilitate aspiring sales executives and shorten their tenure in office. Recommended solutions to the cases can be found in Chap. 13, "The Sales Manager's Manual."

Resolving This Moral Dilemma

One way of dealing with ethics in organizational life is to become a rational schizophrenic—to shift moral codes as you change your social environment. Some of today's typical sales managers recognize the rules of company behavior and adopt them as a code of conduct *only while on the job* or in the firm's work setting. As soon as they leave the competitive confines of the enterprise, each executive adopts a set of principles which is more enlightened—they become compassionate, conscientious human beings again.

The ethical relativity of this rational schizophrenia, however, does not provide a sound basis for a business society nor does it encourage moral integrity. It merely reduces the apparent inner conflict and stress felt by sales executives whose actions are different than their beliefs. In its extreme form, such a rationale leads to corruption and mental infirmity. These unfortunate managers have a talent for keeping their place, doing their duty, taking orders, and turning their collective consciences over to the care of the corporation. In effect, they have "sold their souls to the company store."

Somehow, *you must reconcile and integrate concern for the individual with concern for the organization.* Your long-term mental health demands it. In coping with the moral hazards of sales management, hard and fast guidelines are difficult to come by. Try reading Aristotle's *Ethics*, Jesus' Sermon on the Mount (Matthew 5–7), and other works which will help you to gain moral perspective. Then you must always do the right thing in the right way, regardless of the short-term consequences to your career. As in management development itself, *the ultimate results rest with you.* It's up to you to develop your own inner strength, maturity, and integrated value system to avoid succumbing to rational schizophrenia in your career.

The goal of this chapter is to create an awareness of the human consequences of weak sales management leadership as well as the moral confusion which troubles many new sales executives. Miguel de Cervantes wrote: "My honor is dearer to me than my life." Hopefully, that will also be your leadership philosophy.

Who Motivates the Motivator?

As sales manager, you are the man or woman in the middle; you represent your firm's policy to your mavericks, but you are also their advocate to upper management who makes company policy. Who represents you to both sets of constituents? Nobody. For better or worse, you're strictly on your own. Frustration, role ambiguity, and severe stress can result from this pivotal position in the organizational hierarchy. Your ability to perform your job is affected by a number of factors which are illustrated in Fig. 12-3.

Your effectiveness is determined by the needs of your individual mavericks and the motivational climate of your firm. You must be aware of these variables and their impact on the performance of each of your reps. *Their success is your success.* Managers don't win baseball games, players do. When a team is in a losing streak, however, it's the manager who is replaced, not the players. The same is also true with professional sales managers.

As you will soon learn, sales management is the operant behavior; you only learn it by doing it. You must have the discipline to prepare yourself and the emotional stamina to carry out your assignments. You need the courage to accept the risks of leadership and the flexibility to adapt to a changing environment. The amount of situational control and the quality of your leader/member relationships will determine your ability to influence group behavior. Your job is simplified if your company provides a positive and supportive atmosphere for growth and development. It must give you the resources to do the sales management job and be patient with you as you work your way through the inevitable mistakes which will mark your early endeavors.

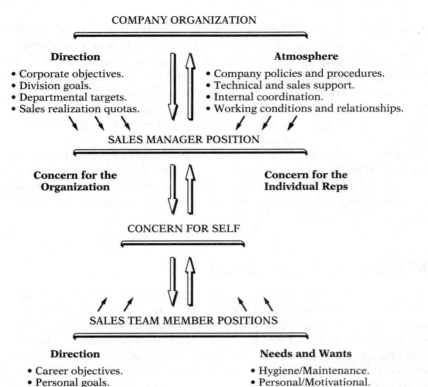

Figure 12-3. The sales manager's organizational dilemma. You are the advocate for your mavericks' feelings and attitudes to upper management while representing company policy and requirements to your salespeople. Who represents your needs and wants to both sets of constituents? Nobody. You are truly the man or woman in the middle. Who motivates the motivator? You do!

Your personal motivation—the desire for power and influence—is the key to your success. If you believe in yourself and want to do the job badly enough, you will prevail, even under the most adverse circumstances. On the other hand, if you believe sales management is nice to have on your résumé but not mandatory, the very first crisis will blow you away. Leadership is not for everyone; few aspire to it or achieve it. But the more adept you become at identifying and satisfying your own personal needs, the higher will be your commitment to your job and your career.

You must rely on your own inner strength and ambition—there is no one else to turn to for help. You're strictly on your own. Small wonder that most new sales managers don't last more than four years on the job. They can't stand the pressures and isolation. If the goal of sales management is really that important to you—if it's your compelling ambition—then you'll get that position and keep it. If not, there's nothing wrong with remaining a rep. Professional salespeople are the true heroes and heroines of every business enterprise.

You Set the Example

This subject was originally introduced in Chap. 10 in a motivational context. Here, it's discussed from a leadership perspective. Every dynamic sales organization mirrors the drive and role behavior of its sales manager. These forceful executives set their groups' objectives, structure the environment, and relentlessly apply pressure for superior performance. Within the established limitations of company policies and procedures, they provide challenging opportunities for growth and development. They liberally praise tasks well done while demanding results—and getting them.

The expectations of your mavericks aren't any different than those of other employees. They want to be compensated fairly, of course, but they also demand competence, integrity, human understanding, inspirational leadership, humane treatment, and a sincere interest in their professional welfare. The desire for firm direction reflects both the unique conditions under which salespeople work and the fact that monetary rewards alone are not a complete performance incentive for them. Even though sales management is a many-faceted job, *only by setting a professional example and giving appropriate recognition can you ever hope to build a viable organization and become a truly effective sales manager.* Here are some tips:

Set a good example, and your team members will take their cues from you. Be of strong character, conviction, and moral integrity. Always do the right thing, regardless of the short-term consequences. It's expected of you. Above all things, a sales manager must be loyal. Double-cross a maverick just once—saying one thing now but doing the exact opposite during a crisis—and you will lose that salesperson's respect and loyalty for evermore. And the word will travel far and wide, both inside and outside your firm. Everyone who hears about that episode (sales team members, fellow executives, customers, and superiors) will think, and rightly so, "If you did it once, you might do it again. You might even do it to me. No, you can't be trusted." Thus, an accumulation of these opinions, based on your daily actions, will set the tone, atmosphere, and spirit of your department. Like the gigantic nose of the French maverick Cyrano de Bergerac, your reputation marches before you by a full half hour. It will show up most noticeably in performance. Nobody wants to follow a weak or deceitful leader. Since loyalty is a two-way street paved with intentions and actions, you must be careful of what you say and the maverick behavior that you reward or punish. Salespeople don't respect a gossip, bigot, or slanderer. They learn less from what you say than from what you do, particularly during difficult dilemmas.

Always be fair and objective in all of your rep relationships. There can be no favorites or scapegoats. Disagreement of itself is not necessarily disloyalty. Allow freedom of expression and the opportunity to take risks. This is the maverick mentality. Mistakes will certainly be made, but valuable lessons can be learned from them. One of the essential attributes of effective sales leaders is enough self-confidence to be able to admit their mistakes and to know that mistakes won't ruin them. Your mavericks must also feel free to admit to an honest mistake without fear of unfair retribution. As long as they come back to you with a plan to remedy the damage, they should have your full support.

Praise your salespeople in public, but criticize them in private. Be constructive, concentrating on correction, not blame. Allow them to retain their sense of dignity. Suggest specific steps to prevent reoccurrence of the same blunder. Forgive, forget, and encourage desired results. Let your sales team members know that you champion their cause. The dedicated advocacy of a sales manager is, to the reps, like a lifeline or safety net.

When appropriate, ask your mavericks for advice and feedback. Let them know that they have a strong voice in your decisions, whenever possible. Make them feel that every organizational problem is *their* problem too. Encourage individual thinking and planning. Make it known that you favor creativity and welcome new ideas. Then follow through on them, giving credit where it's due. This is the essence of manipulator management and the interpersonal key which unlocks your combined talents.

Keep your salespeople informed of new developments at the home office and how they will be affected. Let your staff know where they stand with you and why—no deceptions, please! Advise your close assistants of your plans at their inception. Inform your mavericks, as early as possible, about any changes that will affect them and how. Also tell them about changes that will not affect them but about which they might be concerned.

Always look for opportunities to give recognition, valid criticism, guidance, and fitting challenges. Without a meaningful test, a maverick's potential is never realized, and he or she may become complacent and demotivated. Be fair yet firm in all your dealings with them. Everything that you say, do, or don't do, makes a strong statement about your competence and your character. Try to be consistent. Nobody likes working for a manic depressive.

Evaluate your sales force and submanagers by one criterion only—results.

Therefore, the best way to inspire mavericks to superior performance is to convince them by everything you do, and by your daily attitude and behavior, that you are wholeheartedly supporting them and that they are the heroes and heroines of your company. You have got to *mean it* and *demonstrate it* each and every day.

Chapter 12 Roundup

The Code of the Old West advocates the benevolent use of power and authority to accomplish the legitimate ends of sales management. These issues were addressed in this chapter as well as the ethical issues involved in counseling and disciplining mavericks, evaluating their performance, terminating organizational misfits, and the pressures that new sales managers suffer. After reviewing the moral hazards of executive leadership, professional behavior and personal integrity were emphasized as the best long-term method of building successful sales teams.

Final Words of Advice

Well, pardner, we've come to the end of the trail. Before your author rides off into the sunset, I would like to leave you with these final words of wisdom. They're as timeless as the tumbling tumbleweeds and sagebrush in the Cimarron valley and will always be uplifting and inspirational, even during your darkest days on the range.

If you always do the right thing in the right way, you need never fear the consequences of your actions. Your mavericks will respect you and revere your leadership. When that happens, you will know that you've finally arrived and that the sales management job is yours—golden spurs and all—for as long as you want it. If you believe in yourself and follow the guidelines suggested in this book, you too can become a successful sales manager. Best of luck to you in this worthy endeavor. Now it's time for you to reach into your knapsack, take out your marshal's baton, and start crackin' the whip.

13
The Sales Manager's Manual

It is better to know some of the questions than all of the answers.   JAMES THURBER

Introduction to Solutions

The Sales Manager's Manual—sometimes called the Executive Crib Sheet—contains the answers to all of the case studies, self-probes, and quizzes which were presented in previous chapters. It also contains some western-style advice and current job descriptions for sales managers and mavericks.

Since most companies have sales manuals for their salespeople to refer to, particularly in times of crisis, it's high time that their bosses should also possess such career-saving repositories of information. Perhaps this chapter will extend the longevity of these executives beyond the usual four-year tenure in office.

I hope all readers of *Managing Mavericks* will benefit from reading about this dynamic yet often misunderstood field of management endeavor. If this book enables just one newly appointed sales manager to make the slippery transition from selling to managing and then hang onto her or his job, then I will consider the book to be a resounding success.

Chapter 3: Presidents' Personality Types

Let's begin with the Presidents in Chap. 3 and answer the question Which psychological personality type most frequently makes it to the White House — the top leadership position in the United States? Check Fig. 13-1 for the answer. Exactly half of the dozen Presidents who were analyzed in Chap. 3 were manipulator/facilitators. How many personalities did you get right? What conclusions did you draw from this exercise? The implications are readily apparent. If manipulator/facilitators dominate the most powerful leadership position — the President of the United States — you should work on developing your own manipulator skills. Just don't get caught in the act of manipulating!

Experience indicates that those people who rise to positions of power and influence in most organizations tend to be manipulator/facilitators. The same is also true with sales management. Such managers survive on the job longer than the four-year norm or until they are ready to move on to bigger and better things.

Chapter 4: Completing the Transition

The Case of the Newly Appointed Sales Manager

This case study illustrated many of the mistakes that newly appointed sales managers make because they cannot distinguish between managing and nonmanaging (doing) activities. It focused on short-range planning concerns, such as branch office strategy as related to corporate strategy, the use of available human resources, budgeting and recruiting requirements, and the lack of expressed standards and scheduling. The case study experience was devoid of any long-term considerations, conceptual thinking, or effective leadership.

Other key issues involved in this case study included:

1. Lack of planning or organizing of branch office resources by Tom Greene

2. Poor communications with staff, other departments within the company, and established customers

3. Inept handling of Harvey Blue, the disgruntled senior salesperson and interim branch manager (A sales contest that he was bound to win was definitely *not* the answer.)

Personality type

President	Avoider/abdicator	Achiever/technician	Affiliator/pleaser	Power boss/commander	Manipulator/facilitator
John Calvin Coolidge	X				
Herbert Clark Hoover	X				
Franklin Delano Roosevelt					X
Harry S. Truman		X			
Dwight David Eisenhower					X
John Fitzgerald Kennedy					X
Lyndon Baines Johnson				X	
Richard Milhous Nixon					X
Gerald Rudolph Ford			X		
James Earl (Jimmy) Carter		X			
Ronald Wilson Reagan					X
George Herbert Walker Bush					X
Totals	2	2	1	1	6

Figure 13-1. The Presidents' personality types.

4. The purpose and structure of sales contests (There was no connection with corporate strategy or staff needs.)
5. Greene's lack of administrative skills and penchant for doing rather than managing
6. Personnel problems and personality types
7. Loretta Holiday — sexist issue?
8. Recruitment philosophy and sources
9. Interfacing with other company departments in a coordinated manner
10. Customer complaints and service policy

What Greene did wrong could be an exhaustive list. Here are a few of his failings:

1. He was a doer, not a manager — the Lone Ranger rides again!
2. He did not plan or delegate.
3. He failed to communicate with each member of his staff and his sales support personnel.
4. He failed to address the branch office leadership issue with Harvey Blue.
5. He neglected paperwork and did not require it from his subordinates.
6. He was too egocentric and set a bad example.

Personality profiles of each of the players are as follows:

Tom Greene is a typical power boss/commander.

Harvey Blue is an avoider/abdicator.

Loretta Holiday is an affiliator/pleaser.

Howard LaFlash is a much-too-obvious manipulator/facilitator.

Horace Snodgrass is an achiever/technician.

Answers to the Doing versus Managing Self-Quiz

1. *Doing.* This might be a highly necessary activity, but it is selling not managing. The direct purpose of the call is *not* to get results through others.
2. *Managing.* This is training.
3. *Doing.* This is selling. The direct purpose is *not* to get results through others.

4. *Managing*. This is supervising, assuming that you do not have your mavericks come to you (so you can feel sufficiently needed or productive) for routine solutions to recurring problems which they are capable of handling. It would be counseling if a more formal, planned personal discussion were needed.

5. *Doing*. The actual filling out of the form is clerical. Instructing your secretary how to fill it out would be a managing activity in that it would be delegating.

6. *Managing*. This is motivating.

7. *Doing*. This may be an essential activity, but you are actually performing a personnel function in the same way that you are selling when you call on accounts. When you do the interviewing, you are not currently getting results through others. Deciding to hire someone *after* all the recruiting and selecting has been done would be considered a managing activity.

8. *Managing*. This is communicating for the purpose of control, provided you are doing so to receive possible guidance and direction. Otherwise it may be plain communicating, which anyone does, whether they are a manager or not.

9. *Managing*. This is communicating, probably to develop a selling program, and it could be a form of motivating if your main purpose is to have your maverick participate in developing the idea in order to get later acceptance.

10. *Doing*. You are developing objectives — which is a managing activity — but you are *not* delegating. You are developing objectives by account, which your salespeople should be best qualified to do since they work closely with their accounts. Were you to review the sales objectives of one of your mavericks, you would be managing in that you would undoubtedly be planning part of an overall sales objective to be accomplished by your sales force as a group.

11. *Managing*. This is planning, developing a budget. Fitting the budget in its proper form would be clerical.

12. *Managing*. This is measuring and evaluating.

13. *Managing*. This is probably coordinating, making sure that any price deviations are consistent with an overall plan. This would be a doing activity, however, if procedures and controls could be set up in such a way that certain pricing decisions could be delegated.

14. *Managing*. This is developing the organizational structure.

15. *Doing*. This is a methods engineering function. Deciding to get an improved office layout would be a managing activity.

16. *Managing.* This is developing objectives as well as standards of performance.

17. *Doing.* This is performing a public relations function.

18. *Managing.* This is correcting—taking corrective control action. This could also be considered as the disciplining part of supervision.

19. *Doing.* This might be necessary, but it is the inside part of a salesperson's job. The direct purpose of the telephone call is not to get results *through,* but rather *for,* your mavericks.

20. *Managing.* This is developing a program of marketing strategy to achieve group results.

Chapter 5: Job Descriptions

The following pages contain examples of job descriptions for sales managers and reps. The job description for the position of business development executive is reproduced with the permission of Holly Burgin, senior vice president, Kennedy-Wilson, Inc., Santa Monica, California. The job descriptions for the positions of group sales representative; vice president, sales; and vice president, marketing are produced with the permission of Patricia Merson, PHR, assistant vice president, Human Resources, United Insurance Company of America, Chatsworth, California.

Job Description

Job Title: Business Development Executive

Reports To: Director of Business Development

1. Job Summary:
   A Business Development Executive, as a member of the business development team, has responsibility for client prospecting and qualifying, preparation of proposals, and contract closing; understanding auction marketing, real estate analysis, and financing; establishing and meeting call and contract goals; reporting on client calls; and follow-through in maintaining client relationships and providing customer service.

   A successful Business Development Executive has excellent communication and interpersonal skills, is well organized, flexible, action-oriented, and self-motivated.

(Continued)

2. Specific Duties and Responsibilities
   a. Interview clients to develop a clear understanding of the client's real estate marketing needs and objectives and describe the merits of auction marketing. Evaluate the client's needs to qualify the client as a possible auction marketing prospect. Develop an auction marketing strategy which will meet the client's objectives and prepare a marketing proposal which defines the marketing strategy. Contract with the client to provide auction marketing services.
   b. Consult with the Auction Operations Department during the marketing period and assist, as necessary, to ensure that the needs of the client are met. Provide continued customer service to clients to maintain client relationships and promote future business.
   c. Know and understand all aspects of auction marketing, including possible auction marketing programs, the procedures and services of the Auction Operations Department during the marketing period, auction day, escrow closing, and resale periods.
   d. Analyze real estate markets, accessing local resources for relevant statistical data, and determine the marketability of real estate in target business development geographic regions and specific properties to be auctioned. The analysis will include such factors as market conditions, historical growth trends, economic base analysis, site and neighborhood analysis, survey of comparable product, and capture and absorption rate analysis.
   e. Establish a client call program to develop prospective clients. The program will require establishing call and business development goals and creating an action plan to achieve these goals.
   f. Prepare call reports as required.

Essential Job Profile

1. Team Fit:
   A Business Development team member will have a high level of business and/or real estate sophistication and an interest in sales rather than management; will have contacts in KW's marketing target areas; is creative and able to develop other areas in which to sell KW services.
2. Hidden Job Description:
   A Business Development Executive will have selling experience or an interest and willingness to learn to sell KW services. This person is motivated, enthusiastic, confident, can take rejection and call again; quick, able to develop product knowledge; sensitive, able to determine and understand the needs of the client and deal with fragile egos; and articulate, able to communicate the concept of how and why KW services will work and benefit client.

3. Success Factors:
   a. Able to tackle complicated projects where a tangible result (reward) is not immediately apparent.
   b. Works well and communicates with all types of people, to determine needs for which KW can provide its service.
   c. Works alone and without direction, organizes time well.
   d. Makes a minimum of 20 "in person" calls a month to market KW services.
   e. Is a team player who works in cooperation with other Business Development Executives in developing business, and with Marketing and Auction Operation Department heads in creating and implementing marketing programs.
   f. Is dependable and productive (not a procrastinator).
   g. Has attention to detail in preparing proposals and analyzing real estate.
   h. Is motivated by incentive compensation.
4. Performance Standards:
   A successful Business Development Executive will:
   a. Maintain high standards with regard to presentation, appearance, and ethics, never jeopardizing KW's reputation.
   b. Master product knowledge and develop effective sales skills in no more than one year.
   c. Set goals for developing new business which are specific, measurable, action-oriented, realistic, and trackable.
   d. Be conscientious and dependable, performing as promised and on time, following through on all details.
   e. Adhere to established company procedures in creating and implementing marketing programs.

Chapter 6: Answers to the Lawful Interview Self-Quiz

1. False	9. True
2. True	10. False
3. True	11. True
4. True	12. False
5. True	13. True
6. False	14. False
7. True	15. True
8. False	

JOB DESCRIPTION

Job Title GROUP SALES REPRESENTATIVE					Job Code	
Dept. No.	Dept. Name Sales			Reports To (Title) Regional Sales Manager		
Job Grade 201		Exempt Yes		Job Status RFT		No. Supv. 1 to 3
Written By		Date		Approved By		Date

JOB SUMMARY: (Describe the general purpose of the job, basic responsibilities or goals, including its scope or limitations.)

Primarily responsible for developing new business and retaining existing business.

JOB DUTIES: (List the specific duties or performances necessary to carry out the above-mentioned responsibilities. Include only the most significant duties identifying "what", "why" and "how" and conveying some idea of the frequency of occurrence.)

1. Identify new business opportunities and maintain existing business.

2. Evaluate prospective risks, negotiate with Underwriting regarding rates and options, submit required paperwork.

3. Meet established sales production guidelines.

4. Represent the company in appropriate manner.

INTERACTIONS: (When relevant, describe the relationships & degree of contact with internal & external individuals or groups.)

Extensive interaction with principals of current customers and potential customers. Internal interactions primarily limited to Underwriting Department.

QUALIFICATIONS: (Education requirements, certification or licensing standards, experience and basic knowledge requirements.)

1. Minimum of two years group insurance sales experience.
2. Must have Life and Disability license or equivalent property & casualty license.
3. Strong communication and interpersonal skills.
4. Professional image and demeanor.
5. College degree preferred.

FormWorxJOBDESFR011091

JOB DESCRIPTION

Job Title VICE PRESIDENT, SALES			Job Code 01.1085	
Dept. No. 01-2099	Dept. Name Sales		Reports To (Title) President	
Job Grade X01	Exempt Yes	Job Status RFT	No. Supv. Direct: 5	
Written By	Date	Approved By		Date

JOB SUMMARY: (Describe the general purpose of the job, basic responsibilities or goals, including its scope or limitations.)

Overall responsibility for development of new business and retention of existing business. Establishes sales production guidelines and incentive override programs for sales staff. Trains and motivates sales staff. In concert with Marketing, develops sales strategies to increase Company's marketing share. Serves a key role on the management team, guiding company towards improved profitability.

JOB DUTIES: (List the specific duties or performances necessary to carry out the above-mentioned responsibilities. Include only the most significant duties identifying "what", "why" and "how" and conveying some idea of the frequency of occurrence.)

1. Oversee sales staff, helping identify new business opportunities and maintain existing business, through careful guidance, training and motivational techniques.

2. Establish sales production guidelines which meet company objectives.

3. In concert with Marketing, develop sales strategies and new products to increase the Company's market share.

4. Serve as key member of management team, acting in the Company's best interests, using good judgement and superior business skills to enhance the Company's profitability.

5. Develop annual budget and manage expenditures in a judicious manner.

INTERACTIONS: (When relevant, describe the relationships & degree of contact with internal & external individuals or groups.)

Extensive interaction with principals of current customers and potential customers. Extensive interaction with with executives. Highly visible representative of the Company at industry functions.

QUALIFICATIONS: (Education requirements, certification or licensing standards, experience and basic knowledge requirements.)

1. Four-year degree with Marketing or Business emphasis.
2. Minimum of five years group insurance experience.
3. Strong communication and interpersonal skills.
4. Must be results-oriented, accustomed to pressure and deadlines, preferring to achieve objectives through team effort, rather than alone.
5. Must have innovative and pro-active approach to problem solving.
6. Some familiarity with P.C. software preferred.

FormWorxJOBDESFR011091

JOB DESCRIPTION

Job Title VICE PRESIDENT, MARKETING			Job Code	01.1093	
Dept. No. 01-2599	Dept. Name Marketing		Reports To (Title)	President	
Job Grade X01	Exempt	Yes	Job Status RFT	No. Supv.	Indirect:2
Written By		Date	Approved By		Date

JOB SUMMARY: (Describe the general purpose of the job, basic responsibilities or goals, including its scope or limitations.)

Overall responsibility for development of 1) the Company's strategic marketing plan; 2) new product design and maintenance; 3) special risk products; 4) affiliated business. Serves a key role on the management team, guiding the company towards improved profitability.

JOB DUTIES: (List the specific duties or performances necessary to carry out the above-mentioned responsibilities. Include only the most significant duties identifying "what", "why" and "how" and conveying some idea of the frequency of occurrence.)

1. Develop new special risk and affiliated business; maintain current block of business. May require refinement and/or enhancement of current product/procedures/processes.

2. Develop and maintain lines of business, including life, accident and health, etc.

3. Develop strategic marketing direction for external partially self-funded programs.

4. In conjunction with the Sales Department, design and develop new products.

5. Serve as key member of management team, acting in the Company's best interests, use good judgement and superior business skills to enhance the Company's profitability.

6. Develop annual budget and manage expenditures in a judicious manner.

7. Discharge other responsibilities as required.

INTERACTIONS: (When relevant, describe the relationships & degree of contact with internal & external individuals or groups.)

Extensive interaction with principals of current customers and potential customers. Extensive interaction with executives. Highly visible representative of the Company at industry functions.

QUALIFICATIONS: (Education requirements, certification or licensing standards, experience and basic knowledge requirements.)

1. Four-year degree with Marketing emphasis.
2. Minimum of five years group insurance experience.
3. Strong communication and interpersonal skills.
4. Must be results-oriented, accustomed to pressure and deadlines, preferring to achieve objectives through team effort, rather than alone.
5. Must have innovative and pro-active approach to problem solving.
6. Some familiarity with P.C. software preferred.

FormWorxJOBDESFR011091

If you got them all correct, give yourself a gold star. If you got only one or two wrong, you get a deputy's badge. If you got more than three wrong, you go directly to jail—do not pass go, do not collect $200. The sheriff is after you!

Chapter 9: Answers to the Sales Manager's Self-Quiz

1. *No.* Such a policy, as indicated in Chap. 9, tends to develop an unhealthy dependence on the sales manager. There will, of course, be occasions when you will be needed to help close an order, but most of the time, your rule should be Mavericks are strictly on their own. Otherwise, no professional growth is likely.

2. *No.* Unless you sell encyclopedias or cemetery plots and advocate "canned" sales presentations, the answer to this question is a strong negative. Mavericks need freedom to find and use the close that they are comfortable with and that will also work for each of their individual customers.

3. *No.* A close built around this tactic works only with the greenest of buyers. Experienced customers recognize it for what it is—a ploy. Most clients know that the salesperson can offer an exclusive deal because the clients' competitors have all turned down this product or service proposition. A customer who demands an exclusive deal from a sales rep is in the same situation as the salesperson who tries to use exclusivity to close the sale—at the bottom of the barrel.

4. *Yes.* Even in instances when your sales force is selling well, you should know what methods they are using. It's simply good sales management.

5. *Yes.* Unless yours is an unusual company, periodic training courses, including one on closing techniques, are mandatory. Recent technological developments in your markets, among other things, will strongly affect the close. Remember, many firms are upgrading their purchasing agents and hiring more sophisticated people. This requires that you also retrain and upgrade your staff. To help new salespeople master the complexities of closing, many sales managers now bring together a mix of mavericks who have diverse amounts of experience to their training sessions.

6. *Yes.* It is helpful to have the credit executive or engineering genius on hand when a close is likely to be made. It also prevents the

maverick from making promises that he or she cannot keep or possibly providing information that is erroneous.

7. *Yes.*   Shocking as it is, surveys show that approximately 60 percent of the time salespeople *avoid* attempting to close the sale.

8. *Yes.*   Companies need to ask themselves if their official policies might be making it difficult for their sales force to close orders. A sluggish credit department is a common internal obstacle in making the close, but not the only one. Survey your salespeople to find out.

9. *No.*   A last-minute plea to be allowed to change a bid suggests that Jones deliberately bid high. Moreover, companies that have a "best-price-first" policy are certain not to appreciate Jones's "dramatic" close.

10. *Yes.*   Although this direct tactic will not win this year's Subtle Selling Award, it does lead the buyer to an affirmative reply. It should not be used, of course, until you are certain that the buyer has indeed made the basic decision to buy.

11. *Yes.*   Some firms pay a bonus every quarter on the basis of business booked beyond quota. The salesperson does not have to wait while the customer is billed or the order is actually shipped. Thus, he or she has a real and immediate incentive to close more sales. Unfortunately your chief financial officer might not see it the same way.

12. *Yes.*   Visual aids should be designed so that they include a number of trial closes, such as: "Which size would suit your needs best?" or "What color would you require?" These allow your mavericks to gauge the buyer's interest level and then determine when they can move to a definite close.

13. *Yes.*   Again, a sales rep's time is his or her most valuable possession. Paying a higher incentive when reps save time reminds them of that important factor.

14. *Yes.*   Escorted sales calls are an integral part of field training and coaching. They should be done periodically, not only to police the techniques that your mavericks use but to improve them. The key word in this question is *observe:* A sales manager should refrain from taking over the close if the rep begins to flounder. You should also hold your curbside critique for new reps immediately afterward. Mavericks will welcome escorted account calls if their managers observe the rules. Sales management is a two-way street.

15. *Yes.*   Salespeople who have the power to negotiate are the stronger for it. Just don't let them give the store away!

16. *Yes.*   There is no such thing as only one close. Rather, there are many kinds of closes, each requiring their own special techniques. Also, many calls have closes which are, in effect, steps leading to a subsequent sale — getting the prospect to agree to something, such as a free trial.

17. *Yes.*   Many a sale has been lost when the salesperson who had already won his or her case stayed around too long, thereby giving a problem or some other difficulty the chance to rear its ugly head. Usually affiliator/pleasers are guilty of overstaying their time because of their need to gab.

18. *Yes.*   If they're not interested in money, how in the world are you ever going to motivate these mavericks? Now, it's true that money is not the only motivator, but have you ever met a successful salesperson who wasn't interested in his or her commission check?

19. *Yes.*   If you're not learning and growing all of the time, how can you ever expect your mavericks to do the same? If you checked no, you're probably running, slipping, or sliding downhill at a record pace!

20. *Yes.*   If you got this one wrong, it's back to Chap. 1 for you; obviously, you have not been paying too much attention to the contents of this book.

Chapter 10: Incentive Motivation Suggestions

Whether they will admit it or not, all of your reps crave recognition. Do you know a sales rep who doesn't want to be appreciated for his or her selling efforts? Therefore, you should look for every possible opportunity to recognize accomplishments and stroke egos. Here are some ideas that work. You can add to them from your own personal experience.

Bulletins, Newsletters, and Company House Organs

Constantly publish information about your sales team members and their achievements. Do you presently have:

1. *Maverick of the month?*   A picture of your best salesperson for that month and what he or she did.
2. *Maverick of the year?*   Who is the winner of your firm's Golden Spur Award? How much publicity does he or she get?
3. *Icebreakers?*   First order writers.
4. *Rising stars?*   Rookie reps on the rise.
5. *Rookie of the year?*   Your best new salesperson.

Each of these achievers is also publicly recognized and appreciated at the very next sales meeting with an appropriate award.

Personal Letters

Personal letters and short informal notes can be written by you to your individual sales team members. Use information from your reporting system for their main content. As previously stated, the initial correspondence should come from your company president, welcoming the new recruits aboard. This is followed by a personal, handwritten note from you. Can you imagine the motivational impact on a rookie? They are highly stimulated right from the starting date of their employment with your firm!

Other letters that you can write go to each of your affiliator-, avoider-, and power boss-maverick order producers in which you thank them for getting the business. Not only is this common courtesy but you are also getting rich on override commissions on their sales. Depending upon the number of range riders and their volume of business, you will have to use your own good judgment regarding the frequency and content of these letters.

You could also write individual letters immediately after riding shotgun with a rep in his or her territory or after a coaching, counseling, or field training session or between infrequent visits to distant territories and following appraisal conferences. On special occasions like wedding anniversaries, birthdays, confirmations, bar or bas mitzvahs, graduations, or hospitalizations a greeting card with a short note are in order. Hospital visits are a must! They will never forget your thoughtfulness.

Thus, your mavericks will become aware that you are following their progress with keen interest, that you are observing what they are doing and commenting both pro and con. Besides being a method of control, you are expressing interest in them. As you know, the best way of becoming interesting to others is by being interested in them. Not only are you keeping yourself informed of their activities, which is good management but you are also giving them recognition at every turn.

Contests, Awards, and Incentives

Contests, awards, and various incentives beyond your firm's compensation package are the ultimate tangible expressions of recognition. In putting together contests, there are several time-tested guidelines which will enable you to make them more effective in reaching your objectives. However, if contests are not a part of your overall sales realization plan, they could be self-defeating in the long run. Here are some tips:

1. *Contests should be simple, easily understood by participants, and of short duration—usually not exceeding 30 to 90 days.* Of course, you are going to have your best-salesperson contest on an annual basis, but if your other contests are too long or complicated, they become counterproductive and demotivational.

2. *Challenge your mavericks to do the impossible.* Help them raise their sights and broaden their horizons by stretching them to higher plateaus of order productivity. If your reps are earning $1000 per week, you could establish an exclusive $1500-a-week commission club in which these elite members obtain certain privileges and perks—as well as cash—and a certificate of recognition or a lapel button for their superior efforts.

Most likely, one of your power boss/commander mavericks will break the earnings barrier first and thereby become the founding member of this special club. This will irritate your achiever/technicians, who don't want those "blowhard degenerates" to ever show them up. Both personality types respond well to a challenge because of their highly competitive natures. Soon this competitive spirit, pride, ego, and peer pressure will spur everyone on your staff to become a member of the club. Naturally, your avoider/abdicator reps will be the last to make it. Once they have all qualified for the $1500-a-week club membership, you can then form a $2000-a-week superachiever club and see who the trailblazers will be.

3. *Everybody wins something, if they accomplish something.* Having only one, or a few, big winners and nothing else is a huge demotivator because the majority of your mavericks will "turn off" early in the game when they realize that they cannot win the big prize. Therefore, you should structure your contests so that there is a wide range and variety of prizes which can be claimed, depending on which order-writing plateau an individual salesperson reaches.

4. *Publicize progress of the contestants and winners.* Public praise is where it's at as far as your mavericks are concerned. Focus on their achievements and the exceptional or unique efforts which enabled these participants to win their prizes. How do you think a rep feels when he

or she is *last* in a field of 25 contestants? You know that they are going
to be motivated to rise from the bottom of the list but fast!

5. *Trophies, plaques, certificates, diamond-chip pins, and presidential
awards are worthwhile investments.*   Find as many ways as you possibly can
to offer awards that promote recognition and greatly increase competitive
spirit and peer group pressure for improvement. First develop the award
categories—based on your organization's marketing strategy—and then
decide on the specific awards. Here are some popular favorites:

- Biggest order written this month: the bronze tumbleweed award
- Largest order written this year: the platinum tumbleweed award
- Most new accounts opened this month: the silver six-shooter award
- Most new accounts opened this year: the golden six-shooter award
- Most sales calls made this month: the cowpoke of the month award
- Most sales calls made this year: the cowpoke of the year award
- Best closing ratio (ratio of calls to orders) this month: the silver
  spike award
- Best closing ratio this year: the golden spike award
- Most competitive information obtained: the red kerchief award
- Most dealer sales meetings held this month: the chrome saddle award
- Most dealer sales meetings held this year: the platinum saddle award

The list is endless. You could probably add a few hundred more yourself. If you view these award categories from a conceptual perspective, you
will note that they are the very same criteria that you use to evaluate individual rep job performance. This motivational technique is designed to implement marketing strategy and facilitate employee appraisals.

Naturally, the awards given for monthly achievements should be smaller
than the ones for yearly accomplishments. Remember, the BIGGER the better! Always have the victorious rep's name in LARGE LETTERS on the plaque or
trophy, and make a big fuss about its presentation at your next sales meeting. These awards, if properly conceived and presented, will have as much
importance to a maverick as your own class ring. (Some people—mostly
affiliators—still wear them 20 years after graduation.) Recognition, *recognition,* and more **recognition!** That's the name of the incentive motivation
game.

6. *Get the spouse involved in the sales contest.*   An astute selection of
prizes and frequent letters of contest progress mailed to the rep's
spouse will continue at home the enthusiasm you are creating on the
job. If one of the top prizes is a vacation for two, do you think that the
spouse will allow his or her "maverick" to slack off during a contest?
Now you've created an active accomplice for your motivational schemes.

One firm used the "teaser technique" of sending periodic contest
prize reminders to both spouses during various key intervals. Since one

of the prizes was a trip to Hawaii, each sales contestant received the following sequential motivational mail:

Week 1   A colorful brochure depicting the attractions of Hawaii
Week 2   A flower lei
Week 3   A free dinner-for-two invitation from the hotel
Week 4   An airline reservation form for two with itinerary
Week 5   Half of a one-way ticket to Hawaii
Week 6   A free car rental certificate good for seven days, and a map of the Hawaiian Islands
Week 7   The other half of the one-way airline ticket
Week 8   A claim check for the appropriate prize level

Your contest themes are only limited by your imagination and your incentive budget. The rule should be If everyone produces up to a given standard, they should be rewarded, and the contest should more than pay for itself in terms of increased business. Be careful that contests don't disrupt established working habits and methods. Where possible, they should tie in with, and support, the major overall objectives of your sales department's strategy.

7. *Try other incentives.* Some enlightened company compensation plans have performance bonuses and other incentives built into them. Isn't that what the quota system is supposed to be all about? If your mavericks make quota, they should be rewarded accordingly. Look for every opportunity to encourage extra effort and give appropriate and timely recognition.

A rather novel approach to incentive motivation is the good old Steak and Beans Contest, practiced by old cowpokes in the Old West. Always expert at 'stirring things up' and creating friendly competition with their mavericks, they would divide their range riders into two competing teams for a short-term order-production contest. Upon its conclusion, the results were announced at the local saloon, where both teams were assembled for dinner and a good time. The competing teams were seated across the table from each other — eyeball to eyeball. The winning mavericks got to order steak — which the losers must pay for — while the losers were compelled to eat beans for dinner.

As a former maverick, you have been through enough contests and selling campaigns to know what works and what doesn't. Use your creativity in stimulating your staff to do the impossible (again!) for a short period of time. This is one of the fun parts of a sales manager's job, especially if you're an affiliator/pleaser by nature. Just be careful that your creations don't borrow too many sales from your next fiscal quarter. Traditionally, there is a significant drop in sales volume in the period that follows the conclusion of a big sales contest. Sometimes sand-bagging is a factor. That is why you always have to tie a sales contest into a long-term marketing strategy. As a stand-alone tactic, the sales contest is a sure candidate for Tombstone City.

Chapter 12: The Code of the Old West

Value Systems

This chapter dealt with some of the good, old-fashioned values of the Old West which are timeless in meaning and application. The moral hazards of sales management focused on dilemmas that leaders must resolve while trying to maintain a delicate balance between their concern for the needs of individual mavericks and their concern for organizational goals. Your corporate mandate is to get the job done, but there is also an ethical dimension involved.

You were presented with six short ethical dilemmas in Chap. 12 that represented typical moral issues which confront most managers during their careers. Now that you've had a chance to think about each specific personnel situation and reflect upon the organizational ramifications of your decisions, here are the recommended answers.

Ethical Dilemma Solutions

The right courses of action in Cases 1 and 4 should be obvious to you. In Cases 2, 3, and 5, you have to let those salespeople go. That last used-up maverick, described in Case 6, who is so close to retirement *has earned the right* to stay on the job, even at the expense of efficiency. Although achiever and power boss sales managers might disagree, this rep deserves some kind of gratitude and appreciation for his or her many years of productive service to the firm. This inefficient old-timer could be transferred to a less-demanding position, be given lighter responsibilities, or offered early retirement. As for the others (in Cases 2, 3, and 5), it is your duty to terminate them, no matter how unpleasant this chore might be. Nevertheless, you can do it as decently as possible. Allow them to retain their dignity and self-respect. You owe it to them, you owe it to yourself, and you owe it to the selling profession. You are a professional sales manager!

Words to the Wise

Remember, you cannot tolerate alcoholics, drug addicts, or freeloaders in your ranks. Ignoring these personal problems will surely come back to haunt you in the long run. Poor morale, increased turnover, and the loss of your own source credibility are some of the more predictable results. Legal and ethical considerations dictate that you carefully evaluate each case on an individual basis, offer empathic counseling and professional help — where warranted — while documenting your rep's behavior over an appropriate period of time. Some form of disciplinary action might also be required. If there is no significant improvement or positive behavioral change during this "trial" period (after several official warnings, both verbal and written, have been given), then termination must follow.

Only a weak-willed executive fails to take the necessary action. Nobody wants to follow weak leaders, they are the worst kind of sales managers. Subordinates cannot rely on their judgments because they don't know what these moral weaklings will do in a difficult situation. Much more respect and loyalty are given to tough-minded leaders, the ones who aren't afraid to make those complex and often unpopular decisions, *just as long as they are perceived by their sales team members to be decent, fair, and reliable in their dealings with them.*

The Final Roundup

Firing mavericks is the toughest task you will ever have to do because your executive judgment is on the line. Perhaps you made a mistake in the inception of the sales management process when you hired these unproductive reps, or you failed to give them adequate training and moral support. Maybe you didn't give them a chance, waited too long, or were blinded by the halo effect. Nevertheless, the buck stops on your desk; it's your responsibility to weed out the incompetents and develop the winners. Ultimately, a good sales manager should do the decent thing. You've been through the selling wars; this combat zone is no different. You should know what the decent thing to do is; everyone else does. Remember the immortal words of Ralph Waldo Emerson in this context: "Do not say things. What you are stands over you the while, and thunders so that I cannot hear what you say to the contrary." Therefore, to thine own self be true. Strive to become a professional sales manager who achieves a harmonious balance between the needs of your individual mavericks and the needs of your company. In doing so, always do the right thing in the right way. Then you will be able to effectively manage your mavericks. Good luck and good-bye. Adios, pardner.

Index